Twilight of the Idols
and
The Antichrist

TWILIGHT OF THE IDOLS
AND
THE ANTICHRIST

Friedrich Nietzsche

TRANSLATED BY
THOMAS COMMON

DOVER PUBLICATIONS, INC.
Mineola, New York

DOVER PHILOSOPHICAL CLASSICS

Bibliographical Note

This Dover edition, first published in 2004, is an unabridged republication of the stories "The Twilight of the Idols; or How to Philosophise with a Hammer" and "The Antichrist: An Essay Towards a Criticism of Christianity," excerpted from *The Works of Friedrich Nietzsche*, Vol. XI, published in 1896 by Macmillan and Co., New York.

Library of Congress Cataloging-in-Publication Data

Nietzsche, Friedrich Wilhelm, 1844–1900.
   [Götzendämmerung. English]
   Twilight of the idols ; and, The Antichrist / Friedrich Nietzsche ; translated by Thomas Common.
      p. cm.
  ISBN 0-486-43460-5 (pbk.)
   1. Philosophy. I. Nietzsche, Friedrich Wilhelm, 1844–1900. Antichrist. English. II. Title: Antichrist. III. Title.

B3313.G6713 2004
193—dc22

                                            2003067498

Manufactured in the United States of America
Dover Publications, Inc., 31 East 2nd Street, Mineola, N.Y. 11501

Contents

THE TWILIGHT OF THE IDOLS;
OR
HOW TO PHILOSOPHISE WITH A HAMMER

PREFACE

It requires no little skill to maintain one's cheerfulness when engaged in a sullen and extremely responsible business; and yet, what is more necessary than cheerfulness? Nothing succeeds unless overflowing spirits have a share in it. The excess of power only is the proof of power. — A *Transvaluation of all Values,* that question mark, so black, so huge that it casts a shadow on him who sets it up, — such a doom of a task compels one every moment to run into sunshine, to shake off a seriousness which has become oppressive, far too oppressive. Every expedient is justifiable for that purpose, every "case" is a case of fortune, — *warfare* more especially. Warfare has always been the grand policy of all minds which have become too self-absorbed and too profound: there is healing virtue even in being wounded. A saying, the origin of which I withhold from learned curiosity, has for a long time been my motto:

Increscunt animi, virescit volnere virtus.

Another mode of recuperation, which under certain circumstances is still more to my taste, is *to auscultate idols* . . . There are more idols in the world than realities; that is *my* "evil eye" for this world, it is also my "evil ear" . . . To put questions here for once with a *hammer,* and perhaps to hear as answer that well-known hollow sound which indicates inflation of the bowels, — what delight for one who has got ears behind his ears, — for me, an old psychologist and rat-catcher in whose presence precisely that which would like to remain unheard *is obliged to become audible* . . .

This work also — the title betrays it — is above all a recreation, a sunfreckle, a diversion into the idleness of a psychologist. Is it also perhaps a new warfare? And new idols are auscultated, are they? ... This little work is a *grand declaration of warfare*: and as regards the auscultation of idols, it is no temporary idols, but *eternal* idols which are here touched with a hammer as with a tuning-fork, — there are no older, more self-convinced, or more inflated idols in existence ... Neither are there any hollower ones ... That does not prevent them from being the *most believed in*. Besides people never call them idols, least of all in the most eminent case ...

Turin, 30th September 1888,
the day when the first book of the
Transvaluation of all Values was finished.

FRIEDRICH NIETZSCHE

APOPHTHEGMS AND DARTS

1

Idleness is the parent of all psychology. What! is psychology then a—vice?

2

Even the boldest of us have but seldom the courage for what we really *know*.

3

To live alone, one must be an animal or a God—says Aristotle. The third case is wanting: one must be both—a *philosopher*.

4

Every truth is simple—Is that not doubly a lie?

5

Once for all, there is much I do *not* want to know.—Wisdom sets bounds even to knowledge.

6

We recover best from our unnaturalness, from our spirituality, in our savage moods . . .

7

How is it? Is man only a mistake of God? Or God only a mistake of man?—

8

From the military school of life.—What does not kill me, strengthens me.

9

Help thyself: then everyone else helps thee. Principle of brotherly love.

10

Would that we were guilty of no cowardice with respect to our doings, would that we did not repudiate them afterwards!—Remorse of conscience is indecent.

11

Is it possible for an *ass* to be tragic?—For a person to sink under a burden which can neither be carried nor thrown off? . . . The case of the philosopher.

12

When one has one's *wherefore* of life, one gets along with almost every *how*.—Man does *not* strive after happiness; the Englishman only does so.

13

Man has created woman—out of what do you think? Out of a rib of his God,—his "ideal" . . .

14

What? you are seeking? you would like to decuple, to centuple yourself? you are seeking adherents?—Seek *ciphers!*—

15

Posthumous men—myself, for example—are worse understood than opportune, but are better heard. More strictly: we are never understood—*therefore* our authority . . .

16

Among women.—"Truth? Oh, you do not know truth! Is it not an outrage on all our *pudeurs?*"

17

That is an artist such as I love, modest in his requirements: he really wants only two things, his bread and his art,—*panem et Circen* . . .

18

He who cannot put his will into things, puts at least a *meaning* into them: that is, he believes there is a will in them already. (Principle of "Belief.")

19

What? you choose virtue and a full heart, and at the same time gaze with envy at the advantages of the unscrupulous?—With virtue, however, one *renounces* "advantage" . . . (At the door of an Anti-Semite.)

20

The perfect woman perpetrates literature as she perpetrates a little sin: by way of test, in passing, turning round to look if anybody notices it, and *in order that* somebody may notice it . . .

21

To get ourselves into such conditions only as do not permit us to have feigned virtues; in which, rather, like the rope-dancer on his rope, we either fall, or stand—or escape in safety . . .

22

"Bad men have no songs."[1]—How is it that the Russians have songs?

23

"German *esprit:*" for eighteen years, a *contradictio in adjecto*.

24

By seeking after the beginnings of things people become crabs. The historian looks backwards; he finally *believes* backwards also.

---

[1]Quotation from Seume's Die Gesänge. The correct form is "Rascals have no songs," but "bad men" has become the traditional form of the saying.

25

Contentedness is a prophylactic even against catching cold. Has a woman who knew she was well dressed ever caught cold? I put the case that she was hardly dressed at all.

26

I mistrust all systematisers, and avoid them. The will to system is a lack of rectitude.

27

We think woman deep—why? because we never find any bottom in her. Woman is not even shallow.

28

If a woman possesses manly virtues, she is to be run away from; and if she does not possess them, she runs away herself.

29

"How much the conscience had to bite formerly! what good teeth it had!—And to-day, what is wrong?"—A dentist's question.

30

We seldom commit a single precipitancy. The first time we always do too much. Just on that account we are usually guilty of a second precipitancy—and then we do too little . . .

31

The trodden worm turns itself. That is sagacious. It thereby lessens the probability of being again trodden on. In the language of morality: *submissiveness.*—

32

There is a hatred of lying and dissembling resulting from a sensitive notion of honour; there is also a similar hatred resulting from cowardice inasmuch as lying is *forbidden* by a Divine command. Too cowardly to tell lies . . .

33

How little is required for happiness! The sound of a bag-pipe.— Without music life would be a mistake. The German conceives of God even as singing songs.[1]

34

On ne peut penser et écrire qu'assis (G. Flaubert). There have I got you, nihilist! Sedentary application is the very *sin* against the Holy Ghost. Only thoughts *won by walking* are valuable.

35

There are times when we psychologists become restive like horses: we see our own shadows before us bobbing up and down. The psychologist, to see at all, has to abstract from *himself*.

36

Whether we immoralists do *injury* to virtue?—Just as little as Anarchists do to princes. It is only since princes have been wounded by shots that they sit firmly on their thrones again. Moral: *We must wound morality by our shots.*

37

You run on *ahead?* Do you do so as shepherd? or as an exception? A third case would be that of the deserter . . . *First* question of conscience.

38

Are you genuine? or only a dissembler? A representative? or the represented itself?—Finally, you are merely an imitation of a dissembler . . . *Second* question of conscience.

39

The disillusioned speaks.—I sought for great men; I never found aught but the *apes* of their ideal.

---

[1]An allusion to a song by Arndt, Des Deutschen Vaterland. In the lines:

> So weit die deutsche Zunge klingt
> Und Gott im Himmel Lieder singt

Gott is of course dative; but by a misunderstanding it is traditionally regarded as nominative. Hence the conception of God singing songs over Germany.

40

Are you one who looks on? or one who goes to work? — or one who looks away, and turns aside? . . . *Third* question of conscience.

41

Do you intend to go along with others? or go on ahead? or go by yourself? . . . One must know *what* one intends, and *that* one intends something. — *Fourth* question of conscience.

42

Those were steps for me, I have climbed up beyond them, — to do so, I had to pass them. But it was thought I would make them my resting place . . .

43

Of what consequence is it that *I* am in the right! I *am* too much in the right. — And he who laughs best to-day, will laugh also in the end.

44

Formula of my happiness: A Yea, a Nay, a straight line, a *goal* . . .

THE PROBLEM OF SOCRATES

1

The wisest men in all ages have judged similarly with regard to life: *it is good for nothing*. Always and everywhere we hear the same sound out of their mouth—a sound full of doubt, full of melancholy: full of the fatigue of life, full of resistance to life. Even Socrates said when he died, "To live—that means to be long sick: I owe a cock to Asclepios the saviour." Even Socrates had enough of it.—What does that *prove*? What does it *indicate*? Formerly it would have been said (it has been said indeed and loud enough, and loudest of all by our pessimists!) "Here at all events, there must be something true! The *consensus sapientium* proves the truth."—Are we still to continue talking in such a manner? are we *allowed* to do so? "Here at all events there must be something *diseased*," is *our* answer: those wisest men of all ages, we should look at them close at hand! Were they, perhaps all of them, a little shaky on their legs? latish? tottering? *décadents*? Does wisdom perhaps appear on earth as a raven inspirited by a faint scent of carrion? . . .

2

This irreverence, that the great wise men are *declining types*, first suggested itself to my mind with regard to a case where the strongest prejudices of the learned and the unlearned stood opposed to it: I recognised Socrates and Plato as symptoms of decline, as agencies in Grecian dissolution, as pseudo-Grecian, as anti-Grecian ("The Birth of Tragedy," 1872). That *consensus sapientium*—I understood it better and better—proves least of all that they were correct in that on which they were in accordance: it proves rather that they themselves, those wisest men, were somehow in accordance *physiologically* to take up a position—to have to take up a position—unanimously negative with regard to life. Judgments, valuations with regard to life, for or against, can ultimately never be true: they only possess value as symptoms, they only come into consideration as symptoms,—in themselves such judgments are follies. We must by all means stretch out the hand, and attempt to grasp this surprising *finesse, that the worth of life cannot be estimated*. It cannot be estimated by a living being, because such a one is a party—yea, the very object—in the dispute, and not a judge; it cannot be estimated by a dead person for a different reason.—For a philosopher to see a problem in the worth of life, is really an objection to him, a mark questioning his wisdom, a folly.—What? and all these great wise men—they were not only *décadents*, they were not even wise?—But I come back to the problem of Socrates.

3

Socrates, according to his descent, belonged to the lowest of the people; Socrates was of the mob. One knows, one still sees it one's self, how ugly he was. But ugliness, while it is an objection in itself, is almost a refutation when found among Greeks. Was Socrates Greek at all? Ugliness is often enough the expression of a thwarted development *checked* by cross breeding. Besides, it appears as *deteriorating* development. The anthropologists who are criminologists tell us that the typical criminal is ugly: *monstrum in fronte, monstrum in animo*. But the criminal is a *décadent*. Was Socrates a typical criminal?—At least the famous verdict of a physiognomist, which was so offensive to the friends of Socrates, would not contradict that assumption. A foreigner, who was a judge of countenances, when he passed through Athens, told Socrates to his face that he *was* a *monstrum*—he concealed in himself all the worst vices and passions. And Socrates merely answered, "You know me, Sir."

4

Not only does the confessed dissoluteness and anarchy in his instincts point to *décadence* in Socrates, but the superfœtation of logicality and that *rhachitical malignity* which distinguishes him points in the same direction. Neither must we forget those auditory hallucinations which have wrongly been interpreted in a religious sense, as the "demon of Socrates." Everything is exaggerated in him, everything is *buffo* and caricature; at the same time everything is concealed, reserved, and subterranean.—I try to understand out of what idiosyncrasy the Socratic equation of reason = virtue = happiness originates: that most bizarre of equations, which, in particular, has all the instincts of the older Hellenes opposed to it.

5

With Socrates Greek taste veers round in favour of dialectics. What really happens then? Above all *superior* taste is vanquished, the mob gets the upper hand along with dialectics. Previous to Socrates dialectic manners were repudiated in good society: they were regarded as improper manners, they compromised. The youths were warned against them. Besides, all such modes of presenting reasons were distrusted. Honest things, like honest men, do not carry their reasons in their hands in such fashion. It is indecent to put forth all the five fingers. That which requires to be proved is little worth. All the world over, where authority still belongs to good usage, where one does not "demonstrate" but commands, the dialectician is a sort of buffoon: he is laughed at, he is not taken seriously. Socrates was the buffoon who *got himself taken seriously*. What really happened then?

6

We choose dialectics only when we have no other means. We know we excite mistrust with it, we know it does not carry much conviction. Nothing is easier wiped away than the effect of a dialectician: that is proved by the experience of every assembly where speeches are made. It can only be a *last defence* in the hands of such as have no other weapon left. It is necessary to have to *extort* one's rights; otherwise one makes no use of dialectics. The Jews were therefore dialecticians; Reynard the Fox was a dialectician: what? and Socrates also was one?—

7

—Is the irony of Socrates an expression of revolt? of a moblike resentment? Does he, as one of the suppressed, enjoy his natural ferocity in the dagger-thrusts of syllogism? does he *revenge* himself on the upper classes whom he fascinates?—As a dialectician a person has a merciless instrument in his hand: he can play the tyrant with it; he compromises when he conquers. The dialectician leaves it to his opponent to demonstrate that he is not an idiot; he is made furious, and at the same time helpless. The dialectician *paralyses* the intellect of his opponent.—What? is dialectics only a form of *revenge* with Socrates?

8

I have given to understand what could make Socrates repellent; there is now the more need to explain the fact *that* he fascinated.—That he discovered a new mode of *agon*, of which he became the first fencing-master for the superior circles of Athens—that is one reason. He

fascinated in that he appealed to the agonal impulse of the Hellenes,—
he introduced a variation into the wrestling matches among young
men and youths. Socrates was also a great *erotic*.

9

But Socrates found out somewhat more. He saw *behind* the higher class
of Athenians, he understood that *his* case, the idiosyncrasy of his case,
was no longer exceptional. The same kind of degeneration was prepar-
ing quietly everywhere: old Athens was coming to an end.—And
Socrates understood that all the world had *need* of him,—of his
method, his cure, his special artifice for self-maintenance . . .
Everywhere the instincts were in anarchy; everywhere people were
within an ace of excess: the *monstrum in animo* was the universal danger. "The impulses are about to play the tyrant, we must invent a
counter-tyrant stronger than they" . . . When the physiognomist had dis-
closed to Socrates who he was, a cave of all evil passions, the great iro-
nist uttered another word which gives the key to him. "It is true," he
said, "but I became master over them all." *How* did Socrates become
master over *himself?*—His case was after all only the extreme case, the
most striking case of that which then began to be the universal
trouble—namely, that nobody was any longer master of himself, that
the instincts became mutually *antagonistic*. He fascinated as such an
extreme case,—his fear-inspiring ugliness proclaimed him as such to
every eye; as a matter of course, he fascinated still more as the answer,
the solution, the seeming *cure* of this case.—

10

When it is necessary to make a tyrant out of *reason*, as Socrates did,
there must be considerable danger of something else playing the tyrant.
Rationality was hit upon in those days as a *Saviour*, it was not a matter
of free choice for either Socrates or his "valetudinarians" to be rational,—it was *de rigueur*, it was their *last* expedient. The fanaticism with
which the whole of Greek thought throws itself upon rationality betrays
a desperate situation: they were in danger, they had only one choice:
they had either to go to ruin, or—be *absurdly rational* . . . The moral-
ism of Greek philosophers, from Plato downwards, is pathologically
conditioned; their estimation of dialectics likewise. Reason = virtue =
happiness means merely that we have to imitate Socrates, and put a
permanent *day-light* in opposition to the obscure desires—the day-light
of reason. We have to be rational, clear, and distinct, at any price: every
yielding to the instincts, to the unconscious, leads *downwards* . . .

11

I have given to understand by what means Socrates fascinated: he seemed to be a physician, a Saviour. Is it necessary to expose the error which was involved in his belief in "rationality at any price?"—It is self-deception on the part of philosophers and moralists to think of rising above *décadence* by waging war with it. Rising above it is beyond their power; what they select as an expedient, as a deliverance, is itself only an expression of *décadence:*—they *alter* its expression, they do not do away with itself. Socrates was a misunderstanding; *the whole of improving morality, including Christian morality, has been a misunderstanding* . . . The fiercest day-light, rationality at any price, the life clear, cold, prudent, conscious, without instincts, in opposition to instincts: this itself was only an infirmity, another infirmity, and not at all a way of return to "virtue," to "health," or to happiness. To *have to* combat the instincts—that is the formula for *décadence:* as long as life *ascends*, happiness is identical with instinct.—

12

Has he himself conceived that, this wisest of all self-dupers? Did he say that to himself at the last in the *wisdom* of his courage to meet death? . . . Socrates *wanted* to die:—Athens did not give him the poison cup; *he* gave it to himself; he compelled Athens to give it to him . . . "Socrates is no physician," he said softly to himself: "death is the only physician here . . . Socrates himself was just a chronic valetudinarian" . . .

"REASON" IN PHILOSOPHY

1

People ask me what is all idiosyncrasy in philosophers? . . . For example, their lack of historical sense, their hatred of the very idea of becoming, their Egyptianism. They think they confer *honour* on a thing when they isolate it from its historical relations, *sub specie æterni,*— when they make a mummy out of it. For millenniums philosophers have been handling conceptual mummies only: nothing real has come out of their hands alive. They kill, they stuff, when they adore, these gentlemen, the conceptual idolators,—they become mortally dangerous to everything when they adore. For them death, change, and age, just as well as production and growth, are objections,—refutations even. What is, does not *become*; what becomes, *is* not . . . Now they all believe in what is, with desperation even. As, however, they do not get hold of what is they seek for reasons why it is withheld from them. "There must be a semblance, a deception there, which prevents us perceiving what is: where is the deceiver concealed?"—"We have found it," they cry joyfully, "it is sensuousness! Those senses, which *are also so immoral in other respects,* deceive us with regard to the *true* world. Moral: to escape from the deception of the senses, from becoming, from history, from falsehood,—history is nothing but belief in the senses, belief in falsehood. Moral: denial of all that accords belief to the senses, of all the rest of mankind: that all is 'mob.' To be a philosopher, to be a mummy, to represent monotono-theism by a grave-digger's mimicry!—And above all, away with the *body,* that pitiable *idée fixe* of the senses! afflicted with all the fallacies of logic in existence,—refuted, impossible even, although it is impudent enough to pose as actual" . . .

2

With high reverence I put the name of *Heraclitus* apart from the others. If the mob of the other philosophers rejected the testimony of the senses because they exhibited plurality and alteration, he rejected their

14

testimony because they exhibited things as if they possessed permanence and unity. Heraclitus also did injustice to the senses. They neither deceive in the way the Eleatics believed, nor as he believed,—they
do not deceive at all. What we *make* out of their testimony, that is what
introduces falsehood; for example, the falsehood of unity, the falsehoods of materiality, of substance, of permanence . . . "Reason" is the
cause why we falsify the testimony of the senses. In as far as the senses
exhibit becoming, dissolving, and transforming, they do not deceive . . .
But Heraclitus will always be right in this that being is an empty fiction.
The "seeming" world is the only one; the "true world" has been *deceit-
fully invented* merely . . .

3

—And what fine instruments for observation we possess in our senses!
This nose, for example, of which as yet no philosopher has spoken with
respect and gratitude, is even (in the meantime at least) the most delicate instrument at our disposal: it is able to attest minimum differences
of movement which even the spectroscope cannot attest. At present, we
possess science exactly to the extent we have resolved to *accept* the testimony of the senses,—to the extent we have learned to sharpen them,
furnish them with appliances, and follow them mentally to their limits.
The rest is abortion and not-yet-science: *i.e.* metaphysics, divinity, psychology, and theory of perception. Or formal science, science of symbols; as logic, and that applied form of logic, mathematics. Actuality is
nowhere mentioned in those sciences, not even as a problem; as little
as the question, what value at all such a symbolic convention as logic
possesses.—

4

The *other* idiosyncrasy of philosophers is not less dangerous: it consists
in confounding the last and the first. The products which occur at the
end—alas! for they should not occur at all!—the "highest notions," that
is, the most general, the emptiest notions, the last fume of evaporating
reality are placed by them at the beginning, *as* the begining. This,
again, is but the expression of their mode of doing reverence: the
higher *must* not grow out of the lower, it *must* not be *grown* at all . . .
Moral: everything of the first rank must be *causa sui*. The origin out of
something else is regarded as an objection, as a sign of questionable
value. All highest values are of the first rank, none of the highest notions—the notions of what is, of the unconditioned, of the true, of the
perfect—none of all these can have become; each *must* consequently
be *causa sui*. But none of those highest notions can be unequal either,

they cannot be in disagreement among themselves. They thereby attain their stupendous conception of "God" . . . The last, the thinnest, the emptiest is placed as the first, as cause in itself, as *ens realissimum* . . . Alas, that mankind have had to take seriously the delirium of sick cobweb spinners!—And they have paid dearly for it . . .

5

—Let us finally state, in opposition thereto, how differently *we* (I say courteously we) view the problem of error and seemingness. Formerly, people regarded alteration, mutation, and becoming, generally, as evidence of seemingness, as indications that there could not but be something there which led them astray. At present, on the contrary, we see ourselves entangled in some measure in error, necessitated to error precisely as far as our rational prejudice compels us to posit unity, identity, permanence, substance, cause, materiality, what *is*; however certain we are, by means of a strict recalculation of the account, that the error is found there. It is just the same here as with the motion of the sun. There, our eyes are the agencies through which error constantly operates, here it is our *language*. In its origin, language belongs to the age of the most rudimentary form of psychology: we come into the midst of a gross fetich system when we call up into consciousness the fundamental presuppositions of linguistic metaphysics (*i.e.* the presuppositions of "*reason*"). This system sees everywhere actors and action; it believes in will as cause in general; it believes in the "ego," in the ego as being, in the ego as substance; and it *projects* the belief in the ego-substance on to everything—it first *creates* thereby the conception "thing" . . . Being is everywhere thought into, and *foisted upon* things, as cause; it is only from the conception "ego" that the derivative conception of being follows . . . At the commencement there is the great bane of error,—that will is something which *acts*—that will is a *faculty* . . . We now know that it is merely a word . . . Very much later, in a world a thousand times better enlightened, the *certainty*, the subjective *assurance* in handling the categories of reason, came, all of a sudden, to the consciousness of philosophers: they concluded that those categories could not have their origin in experience—for the whole of experience, they said, was in opposition to them. *Consequently, whence do they originate?*—And in India, as in Greece, the same mistake has been fallen into: "we must once have belonged to a higher world (instead of *one very much lower*, which would have been the truth!), we must have been Divine, *for* we possess reason!" In fact, nothing has hitherto had a more naïve convincing power than the error of being, as it was formulated, for example, by the Eleatics; for it has in its favour every word, every sentence which we utter!—The opponents of the Eleatics likewise yielded to the misleading influence of their concept of being; Democritus among others, when he devised his atom . . . "Reason" in language: oh what a deceitful old female! I fear we do not get rid of God, because we still believe in grammar . . .

6

People will be thankful if I compress into four theses such an essential and such a new insight. I thereby make it more easily understood; I thereby challenge contradiction.

First Proposition. The grounds upon which "this" world has been designated as seeming, rather establish its reality,—*another* kind of reality cannot possibly be established.

Second Proposition. The characteristics which have been assigned to the "true being" of things are the characteristics of non-being, of *nothingness;*—the "true world" has been built up out of the contradiction to the actual world: a seeming world in fact, in as far as it is merely an illusion of *moral optics.*

Third Proposition. To fable about "another" world than this has no meaning at all, unless an instinct of calumniation, disparagement, and aspersion of life is powerful in us: if that be the case we take *revenge* on life, with the phantasmagoria of "another," a "better" life.

Fourth Proposition. To separate existence into a "true" and a "seeming" world, either in the manner of Christianity, or in the manner of Kant (who was a *wily* Christian at last), is only a suggestion of *décadence,*—a symptom of *deteriorating* life . . . That the artist values appearance more than reality is no objection against this proposition. For here "appearance" means reality *once more*, only select, strengthened, and corrected reality . . . The tragic artist is *no* pessimist,—he rather *says yea,* even to all that is questionable and formidable; he is *Dionysian* . . .

HOW THE "TRUE WORLD" FINALLY BECAME A FABLE

HISTORY OF AN ERROR

1. The true world attainable by the wise, the pious, and the virtuous man,—he lives in it, *he embodies it.*
   (Oldest form of the idea, relatively rational, simple, and convincing. Transcription of the proposition, "I, Plato, *am* the truth.")
2. The true world unattainable at present, but promised to the wise, the pious, and the virtuous man (to the sinner who repents).
   (Progress of the idea: it becomes more refined, more insidious, more incomprehensible,—it *becomes feminine*, it becomes Christian.)
3. The true world unattainable, undemonstrable, and unable to be promised; but even as conceived, a comfort, an obligation, and an imperative.
   (The old sun still, but shining only through mist and scepticism; the idea become sublime, pale, northerly, Kœnigsbergian.)
4. The true world—unattainable? At any rate unattained. And being unattained also *unknown.* Consequently also neither comforting, saving, nor obligatory: what obligation could anything unknown lay upon us?
   (Grey morning. First yawning of reason. Cock-crowing of Positivism.)
5. The "true world"—an idea neither good for anything, nor even obligatory any longer,—an idea become useless and superfluous, *consequently* a refuted idea: let us do away with it!
   (Full day; breakfast; return of *bon sens* and cheerfulness; Plato blushing for shame, infernal noise of all free intellects.)
6. We have done away with the true world: what world is left? perhaps the seeming? . . . But no! *in doing away with the true, we have also done away with the seeming world!*
   (Noon; the moment of the shortest shadow; end of the longest error; climax of mankind; *INCIPIT ZARATHUSHTRA.*)

MORALITY AS ANTINATURALNESS

1

All passions have a time when they are fatal only, when, with the weight of their folly, they drag their victim down; and they have a later, very much later period, when they wed with spirit, when they are "spiritualised." Formerly, people waged war against passion itself, on account of the folly involved in it, they conspired for its annihilation,— all old morality monsters are unanimous on this point: "*il faut tuer les passions.*" The most notable formula for that view stands in the New Testament, in the Sermon on the Mount, where, let us say in passing, things are not at all regarded *from an elevated point of view*. For example, it is there said with application to sexuality, "If thine eye offend thee, pluck it out." Fortunately no Christian acts according to this precept. To *annihilate* passions and desires merely in order to obviate their folly and its unpleasant results appears to us at present simply as an acute form of folly. We no longer admire the dentist who *pulls out* the teeth, that they may no longer cause pain. It may be acknowledged, on the other hand, with some reasonableness that, on the soil out of which Christianity has grown, the notion of a "*spiritualisation*" of passion could not at all be conceived. The primitive Church, as is well known, battled *against* the "intelligent" in favour of the "poor in spirit:" how could we expect from it an intelligent war against passion?—The Church fights against passion with excision in every sense: its practice, its "cure" is *castration*. It never asks, "How to spiritualise, beautify, and deify a desire?"—it has, at all times, laid the emphasis of discipline upon extermination (of sensuality, of pride, of ambition, of avarice, of revenge).—But to attack the passions at the root means to attack life itself at the root: the praxis of the Church is *inimical to life* . . .

2

The same means, castration, extirpation, is instinctively chosen in the struggle with a desire by those who are too weak of will and too degen-

19

erate to be able to impose due moderation upon themselves; those natures, which, to speak with a simile (and without a simile), need *la
Trappe*,—any definitive declaration of hostility, a *gap* between themselves and a passion. The radical means are indispensable only to the
degenerate: weakness of will, or to speak more definitely, the incapa-
bility of *not* reacting in response to a stimulus, is itself merely another
form of degeneration. Radical hostility, deadly hostility against sensuality is always a critical symptom; one is thereby justified in making con-
jectures with regard to the general condition of such an extremist.
Moreover, that hostility, that hatred, only reaches its height when such
natures no longer possess sufficient strength for a radical cure,—for ab-
juring their "devil." Survey the whole history of priests and philosophers, that of artists also included, and you will see: the most virulent
attacks on the senses are *not* made by the impotent, *nor* by ascetics, but
by impossible ascetics, those who would have required ascetic life . . .

3

The spiritualisation of sensuousness is called *love*; it is a grand triumph
over Christianity. Our spiritualisation of *hostility* is another triumph. It
consists in profoundly understanding the importance of having enemies: in short, in acting and reasoning the reverse of the former acting
and reasoning. The Church always wanted to exterminate its enemies:
we, the immoralists and Anti-Christians, see our advantage in the existence of the Church . . . In political matters also hostility has now become more spiritualised,—much more prudent, much more critical,
much *more forbearing*. Almost every party conceives that it is advanta-
geous for its self-maintenance if the opposite party does not lose its
power; the same is true in grand politics. A new creation especially, *e.g.*
the new Empire, has more need of enemies than of friends: it is only
in opposition that it feels itself indispensable, that it *becomes* indispensable . . . Not otherwise do we comport ourselves towards the "inner
enemy;" there also we have spiritualised hostility, there also we have
understood its *worth*. People are *productive* only at the cost of having
abundant opposition; they only remain *young* provided the soul does
not relax, does not long after peace . . . Nothing has become more alien
to us than the desirability of former times, that of "peace of soul,"
Christian desirability; nothing makes us less envious than the moral
cow and the plump comfortableness of good conscience. One has renounced *grand* life, when one has renounced war . . . In many cases,
to be sure, "peace of soul" is merely a misunderstanding—something
different, which does not just know how to name itself more honestly.
Without circumlocution and prejudice let us take a few cases. "Peace

of soul" may, for example, be the mild radiation of a rich animality into the moral (or religious) domain. Or the beginning of fatigue, the first shadow which the evening—every sort of evening—casts. Or a sign that the air is moist, that southern winds arrive. Or unconscious gratitude for a good digestion (occasionally called "charitableness"). Or the quieting down of the convalescent to whom all things have a new taste and who is waiting in expectancy. Or the condition which follows upon a full gratification of our ruling passion, the agreeable feeling of a rare satiety. Or the senile weakness of our will, of our desires, of our vices. Or laziness, persuaded by conceit to deck itself out in moral guise. Or the attainment of a certainty, even a dreadful certainty, after long suspense and torture through uncertainty. Or the expression of proficiency and mastery in doing, creating, effecting, and willing, tranquil breathing, *attained* "freedom of will" . . . *Twilight of the Idols:* who knows? perhaps also just a modification of "peace of soul" . . .

4

—I formulate a principle. All naturalism in morality, *i.e.* all *healthy* morality, is ruled by an instinct of life,—some command of life is fulfilled by adopting a certain canon of "thou shalt" and "thou shalf not," some hindrance and inimical agency on the way of life is thereby removed. *Antinatural* morality, on the other hand (*i.e.* almost every morality which has hitherto been taught, reverenced, and preached), directs itself straight *against* the instincts of life,—it *condemns* those instincts, sometimes secretly, at other times loudly and insolently. Saying that "God looks on the heart," it negatives the lowest and the highest vital desirings, and takes God as the *enemy of life* . . . The saint in whom God finds his highest satisfaction is the ideal castrate . . . Life is at an end where the "Kingdom of God" begins . . .

5

If the wickedness of such a mutiny against life as has become almost sacrosanct in Christian morality has been understood, something else has, fortunately, been understood besides: the uselessness, the unreality, the absurdity, and the *deceitfulness* of such a mutiny. For a condemnation of life on the part of a living being is ultimately just the symptom of a certain kind of life: the question whether rightly or wrongly is not at all raised thereby. We would have to have a position *outside of* life, and yet have to know it as well as each and all who have lived it, to be authorised to touch on the problem of the *worth* of life at all: sufficient reason to convince us that for us the problem is inaccessible. Speaking of values, we speak under the influence of the inspiration and the optics of life: life itself compels us to fix values; life itself values through us, *when* we fix values . . . It follows therefrom that even that *antinaturalness in morality* (which takes God as the counter-principle and condemnation of life) is but an evaluation of life,—of *which* life? of *which* kind of life?—But I have already given the answer: of declining, weakened, fatigued, condemned life. Morality, as it has hitherto been understood—as it was last formulated by Schopenhauer as "denial of will to life"—is the actual *décadence instinct* which makes out of itself an imperative: it says, "Perish!"—it is the valuation of the condemned . . .

6

Let us consider in the last place what *naïveté* it manifests to say, "Man *ought* to be so and so!" Reality exhibits to us an enchanting wealth of types, the luxuriance of a prodigality of forms and transformations; and some paltry hod-man of a moralist says with regard to it, "No! man ought to be different!" . . . He even knows *how* man ought to be, this parasite and bigot: he paints himself on the wall and says, *"Ecce homo!"* . . . But even if the moralist directs himself merely to the individual and says, "You ought to be so and so," he still continues to make himself ridiculous. The individual, in his antecedents and in his consequents, is a piece of fate, an additional law, an additional necessity for all that now takes place and will take place in the future. To say to him, "Alter thyself," is to require everything to alter itself, even backward also . . . And in reality there have been consistent moralists; they wanted man to be otherwise,—namely, virtuous; they wanted him fashioned in their likeness, as a bigot: For that purpose they *denied* the world. No insignificant madness! No modest form of presumption! . . . Morality, in as far as it *condemns* in itself, and not from regards, considerations, or purposes of life, is a specific error with which we must have no sympathy, it is a *degenerate idiosyncrasy* which has caused an unutterable amount of harm! . . . We others, we immoralists, on the contrary, have opened our hearts for the reception of every kind of intelligence, conception, and *approbation*. We do not readily deny, we glory in being *affirmative*. Our eyes have always opened more and more for that economy which still uses and knows how to use for its advantage all that is rejected by the holy delirium of the priest, of the *diseased* reason of the priest; for that economy in the law of life which even derives advantage from the offensive species of bigots, priests, and the virtuous,—*what* advantage?—But we immoralists ourselves are the answer . . .

THE FOUR GREAT ERRORS

1

Error of confounding cause and effect. — There is no more dangerous error than *confounding consequence with cause:* I call it the intrinsic depravity of reason. Nevertheless, this error belongs to the most ancient and the most modern habitudes of the human race: it is consecrated even among us; it bears the names, "religion" and "morality." It is contained in *every* proposition which religion and morality formulate: priests, and legislators in morals, are the originators of this depravity of reason. I take an example: everybody knows the book of the celebrated Cornaro, in which he recommends his spare diet as a recipe for a long and happy life, — for a virtuous life also. Few books have been read so much; even yet many thousand copies of it are annually printed in England. I believe hardly any book (the Bible by right excepted) has caused so much harm, has *shortened* so many lives, as this well-meant curiosity. The source of this mischief is in confounding consequence with cause. The candid Italian saw in his diet the *cause* of his long life, while the pre-requisite to long life, the extraordinary slowness of the metabolic process, small consumption, was the cause of his spare diet. He was not at liberty to eat little or much; his frugality — was *not* of "free will;" he became sick when he ate more. He who is not a carp, however, not only does well to eat *properly*, but is obliged to do so. A scholar of *our* day, with his rapid consumption of nerve-force, would kill himself with the *régime* of Cornaro. *Crede experto.* —

2

The most universal formula which lies at the basis of every religious and moral system is, "Do so and so, refrain from so and so — then you will be happy! In case of disobedience . . ." Every system of morality, every religion *is* this imperative; — I call it the great original sin of reason, *immortal unreason.* In my mouth, that formula transforms into its inversion — the *first* example of my "Transvaluation of all Values": a

23

man well constituted, a "fortunate man," *has* to do certain actions, and instinctively avoids other actions; he introduces the arrangement which he represents physiologically into his relations to men and things. In a formula: his virtue is the *result* of his good fortune . . . Long life and an abundant posterity are *not* the rewards of virtue: the very slowing of the metabolic process, which among other things, has in its train a long life, an abundant posterity, in short, *Cornarism* is rather virtue itself.— The Church and morality say that "a family, a people, is ruined through vice and luxury." My *re-established* reason says that when a people is perishing, when it degenerates physiologically, vice and luxury *follow* therefrom (*i.e.* the need of continually stronger and more frequent stimulants, such as every exhausted nature is acquainted with). This young man becomes pale and withered at an early age. His friends say that this or that sickness is the cause of it. My opinion is *that* the fact of his becoming sick, the fact of his inability to withstand the sickness, was from the first the consequence of an impoverished life and hereditary exhaustion. The newspaper readers say that this party ruins itself by such and such an error. My *higher* politics say that a party which commits such errors is at its end—its instincts are no longer to be relied upon. Every error, whatever it may be, is the result of degeneration of instinct, disgregation of will: we thereby almost define the *bad*. Everything *good* is instinct—and consequently easy, necessary, free. Trouble is an objection, the God is typically distinguished from the hero (in my language: the *light* feet are the first attribute of Divinity).

3

Error of false causality.—It was always believed that we knew what a cause was; but whence did we derive our knowledge, or, more exactly, our belief that we knew about the matter? Out of the domain of the celebrated "inner facts," none of which have hitherto proved themselves actual. We believed that we ourselves acted causally in the exercise of will; we thought *there*, at least, we had *surprised* causality *in the very act*. In like manner people did not doubt that all the *antecedentia* of an action, its causes, were to be sought in consciousness, and would be rediscovered therein, if sought for—as "motives:" for otherwise man would not have been free to act, he would not have been answerable *for* his actions. Finally, who would have disputed that a thought is caused? that the ego causes the thought? . . . Of those three "inner facts" by which causality appeared to be guaranteed, the first and most convincing is that of *will as a cause*; the conception of consciousness ("spirit") as cause, and later still that of the ego (the "subject") as cause,

are merely posthumous and have originated when causality, derived
from will, was established as a given fact—as *empiricism* . . . In the
meantime we have changed our mind. We no longer believe a word of
it all. The "inner world" is full of phantoms and will-o'-the-wisps: will
is one of them. Will no longer *moves* anything, consequently also it no
longer explains anything,—it merely *accompanies* proceedings, it can
also be absent. The so-called "motive"—another error. Merely a surface phenomenon of consciousness, some accompaniment of an act,
which *conceals* the *antecedentia* of an act *rather* than manifests them.
And above all the ego! It has become a fable, a fiction, a play upon
words; it has altogether ceased to think, to feel, and to will! . . . What
follows therefrom? There are no spiritual causes at all! The whole of
the alleged empiricism that seemed to be in their favour has gone to
the devil! That follows therefrom!—And we had made a fine abuse of
that "empiricism:" we had *created* the world on that basis, as a world of
causes, as a world of will, as a world of spirit. The oldest psychology and
the longest maintained has here been at work, it has really done nothing else. According to this psychology, every occurrence was an action,
every action was the result of a will; the world, according to it, became
a plurality of acting agents; an acting agent (a "subject") was insinuated
into every occurrence. Man has projected outside himself his three
"inner facts," that in which he believed firmest of all, will, spirit, and
the ego,—he only derived the conception of being from the conception of the ego, he posited "things" as existing according to his own likeness, according to his conception of the ego as cause. What wonder
that later on he always just rediscovered in things *what he had concealed in them?*—The thing itself, we repeat, the conception of a
thing—a reflection merely of the belief in the ego as a cause . . . And
even your atom, Messrs. the Mechanists and Physicists, how much
error, how much rudimentary psychology, yet remains in your atom!—
Not to speak of the "thing in itself," the *horrendum pudendum* of metaphysicians! The error of spirit as a cause, confounded with reality! And
made the measure of reality! And called *God!*—

4

Error of imaginary causes.—To start from the dream. For a definite sensation resulting, for example, from the distant shot of a cannon, there
is a cause subsequently foisted on (often quite a little romance in which
the dreamer himself is the hero). The sensation, in the meantime, per-
sists as a sort of resonance; it waits, as it were, until the causal impulse
permits it to move into the foreground of consciousness—now *no*
longer as a fortuitous incident, but as "meaning." The cannon shot

appears in a *causal* connection, with a seeming inversion of time. The later, the motivation, is first realised, often with a hundred details which pass like lightning; the shot *follows* . . . What has happened? The ideas *generated* by a certain bodily state were mistaken for its cause. — As a matter of fact, we do just the same when we are awake. Most of our general sensations — every sort of check, pressure, tension, or explosion in the play and counterplay of organs, especially the condition of the *nervus sympathicus* — excite our causal impulse; we want a *reason* for feeling *so and so,* — for feeling ill or well. It never suffices us merely to establish the fact *that* we feel so and so: we only acknowledge this fact — we only become *conscious* of it — *when* we have furnished it with some kind of motivation. — The recollection, which in such cases becomes active without our being aware of it, calls up earlier conditions of the same kind, and the causal interpretations associated with them, — *not* their causality. The belief that the associated ideas, the accompanying proceedings of consciousness, have been the causes, is also, to be sure, called up by recollection. There thus originates an *habituation* to a fixed causal interpretation, which, in truth, checks the *investigation* of causes, and even excludes it.

5

Psychological explanation. — To trace back something unknown to something known, relieves, quiets, and satisfies, besides giving a sensation of power. There is danger, disquiet, and solicitude associated with the unknown, — the primary instinct aims at *doing away with* these painful conditions. First principle: any explanation whatsoever is better than none. Since, after all, it is only a question of wanting to get rid of depressing ideas, people are not specially careful about the means for getting rid of them: the first conception, by which the unknown declares itself to be something known, is so pleasing that it is "taken as true." Proof of *desire* ("power") as criterion of truth. — The causal impulse is thus conditioned and excited by the feeling of terror. The "why" is intended, if possible, not so much for furnishing the cause on its own account, as for furnishing a *species of cause* — a quieting, liberating, alleviating cause. The first result of this need is that something already *known*, something experienced, something inscribed in the memory, is assigned as cause. The new, the unexperienced, the strange are excluded from being a cause. — Thus there is not only a mode of explanation sought for as cause, but a *select* and *privileged* mode of explanation — that by means of which the feeling of the strange, the new, and the unexperienced, has been most quickly and most frequently got rid of, — the *most* common explanations. — Result: a particular mode of assigning causes preponderates more and more, concentrates itself into a system, and finally becomes *predominant, i.e.* simply excluding *other* causes and explanations.—The banker immediately thinks of "business," the Christian of "sin," and the girl of her love.

6

The whole domain of morality and religion comes under this conception of imaginary causes. —"Explanation" of *unpleasant* general feelings:— They are determined by beings hostile to us (evil spirits: the most striking case—mistaking hysterics for witches). They are determined by conduct not to be approved of (the feeling of "sin," of "sinfulness," foisted on to a physiological unpleasantness—one always finds reasons for being discontented with one's self). They are determined as punishments, as a requital for something we should not have done, for *being* otherwise than we ought to be (audaciously generalised by Schopenhauer into a thesis in which morality appears undisguised, as the actual poisoner and calumniator of life: "every sore pain, whether bodily or mental, indicates what we deserve, for it could not come upon us, unless we deserved it." *Welt als Wille und Vorstellung* 2, 666). They are determined as consequences of inconsiderate actions, which turn out badly (the emotions, the senses, assigned as cause, as "guilty;" states of physiological trouble explained as "deserved" by means of *other* states of trouble).—Explanations of *pleasant* general feelings:— They are determined by trust in God. They are determined by the consciousness of good conduct (so-called "good conscience," a physiological condition sometimes so like a good digestion as to be mistaken for it). They are determined by the successful issue of undertakings (a *naïve* fallacy: the successful issue of an undertaking does not at all produce any pleasant general feelings in a hypochondriac, or in a Pascal). They are determined by faith, hope, and love—the Christian virtues.— In fact, all these presumed explanations are *resulting* conditions, and as it were translations of pleasant and unpleasant feelings into a false dialect: we are in a condition to be hopeful, *because* our fundamental physiological feeling is again strong and rich; we trust in God, because the feeling of fulness and of strength gives us peace.—Morality and religion belong entirely to the *Psychology of Error:* in every individual case cause and consequence are confounded; or truth is confounded with the result of what is *believed* to be true; or a condition of consciousness is confounded with the causation of this condition.

7

Error of free will. —Now we have no longer sympathy with the notion of "free will:" we know only too well what it is—the most disreputable of all theological devices for the purpose of making men "responsible" in their sense of the word, that is, for the purpose of *making them dependent on theologians* . . . Here, I only give the psychology of the process of making men responsible.—Wherever responsibility is sought after, it is usually the instinct *prompting to punish and condemn* which seeks after it. Becoming has been divested of its innocence when any mode of being whatsoever is traced back to will, to purposes, or acts of responsibility: the dogma of will has principally been invented for the purpose of punishment, *i.e.* with the *intention of finding guilty*. The whole of old psychology, will-psychology, would have been impossible but for the fact that its originators (the priests at the head of the old commonwealths) wanted to create for themselves a *right* to impose punishment—or a right for God to do so . . . Men were imagined to be "free," in order that they might be condemned and punished,—in order that they might become *guilty*: consequently every activity *had to be* thought of as voluntary, the origin of every activity *had to be* thought of as residing in consciousness (whereby the most *absolute* false-coinage *in psychologicis* was made a principle of psychology itself . . .). Now when we have entered upon a movement in the *opposite* direction, when we immoralists especially endeavour with all our power to remove out of the world the notions of guilt and punishment, and seek to cleanse psychology, history, nature, social institutions and sanctions from these notions, there is not in our eyes any more fundamental antagonism than that of theologians, who, with the notion of a "moral order of the world," go on tainting the innocence of becoming with "punishment" and "guilt." Christianity is the hangman's metaphysics.

8

What alone can *our* teaching be?—That no one *gives* a man his qualities, neither God, nor society, nor his parents and ancestors, nor *he himself* (the latter absurd idea here put aside has been taught as "intelligible freedom" by Kant, perhaps also by Plato). *No one* is responsible for existing at all, for being formed so and so, for being placed under those circumstances and in this environment. His own destiny cannot be disentangled from the destiny of all else in past and future. He is *not* the result of a special purpose, a will, or an aim, the attempt is *not* here made to reach an "ideal of man," an "ideal of happiness," or an "ideal of morality;"—it is absurd to try to *shunt off* man's nature towards some goal. We have invented the notion of a "goal:" in reality a goal is *lacking* . . . We are necessary, we are part of destiny, we belong to the whole, we *exist* in the whole,—there is nothing which could judge, measure, compare, or condemn our being, for that would be to judge, measure, compare, and condemn the whole . . . *But there is nothing outside of the whole!—This only is the grand emancipation:* that no one be made responsible any longer, that the mode of being be not traced back to a *causa prima,* that the world be not regarded as a unity, either as sensorium or as "spirit;"—it is only thereby that the *innocence* of becoming is again restored . . . The concept of "God" has hitherto been the greatest *objection* to existence . . . We deny God, we deny responsibility by denying God: it is only *thereby* that we save the world.—

THE "IMPROVERS" OF MANKIND

1

It is known what I require of philosophers—namely, to take up their position *beyond* good and evil, *to be superior* to the illusion of moral sentiment. This requirement follows from a principle which I formulated for the first time,—namely, *that there is no such thing as a moral fact.* Moral sentiment has this in common with religious sentiment: it believes in realities which do not exist. Morality is only an interpretation of certain phenomena, or, more definitely, a *mis*interpretation of them. Moral sentiment belongs, like religious sentiment, to a stage of ignorance in which the very notion of the real, the distinction between the real and the imaginary, is yet lacking: accordingly, at such a stage of intellectual development, "truth" designates nothing but what we at present call "fancies." In so far the moral sentiment is never to be taken literally: as such it contains nothing but absurdity. As *semeiotic*, however, its worth remains inestimable: it reveals, at least to the initiated, the most important realities of civilisations, and internal operations which did not *know* sufficient to "understand" themselves. Morality is merely sign language, merely symptomatology; one has to know beforehand *what* it deals with, in order to derive advantage from it.

2

A first example, and quite preliminary. At all times efforts have been made to "improve" human beings: it is that above all things which has been termed morality. The most different tendencies, however, are concealed under the same name. The *taming* of animal man, as well as the *breeding* of a particular species of human beings, has been called "improving;" only these zoölogical *termini* express realities,—realities, indeed, of which the typical "improver," the priest, knows nothing— does not *want* to know anything . . . To call the taming of an animal the "improving" of it, sounds almost like a joke to our ears. Anybody who knows what goes on in menageries will be doubtful about the "improving" of animals there. They are weakened, they are made less mischievous, they become *sick* by the depressing emotion of fear, by pain, wounds, and hunger.—It is precisely the same with tamed man whom the priest has "improved." In the early Middle Ages, when in fact the Church was a menagerie more than anything else, the finest specimens of the "blond beast" were everywhere pursued—the distinguished Germanics for example were "improved." Afterwards, however, how did such a Germanic look when "improved," when seduced into the monastery? Like a caricature of man, like an abortion: he had become a "sinner," he stuck fast in the cage, he had got shut up in the midst of nothing but frightful notions . . . And now he lay there, sick, miserable, ill-disposed towards himself; full of hatred against the vital instincts, full of suspicion with regard to everything still strong and happy. In short, a Christian . . . Physiologically explained: in combat with the animal, the only means for making it weak *can* be to sicken it. The Church understood this: it *ruined* man, it weakened him,—but it claimed to have "improved" him . . .

3

Let us take the other case of so-called morality, the case of *breeding* a distinct race and species. Indian morality, sanctioned into a religion as the "Law of Manu," furnishes the grandest example. The task is here set to breed no fewer than four races all at once: a priestly race, a warrior race, a trading and agricultural race, and, finally, a menial race, the Sudras. Here we are obviously no longer among the tamers of animals; a race of men a hundred times milder and more reasonable is presupposed, even to conceive the plan of such a system of breeding. One recovers breath on stepping into this healthier, higher, and *wider* world out of the sickroom air and prison air of Christianity. How paltry is the New Testament in comparison with Manu, what a bad odour it has!— But that organisation also required to be *formidable*,—not, this time, in combat with the beast, but with *its* own antithesis, the non-caste man, the mishmash man, the Chandala. And again it had no other expedient for making him harmless, for making him weak, except making him *sick*,—it was the struggle with the "great number." Perhaps there is nothing more repugnant to our feelings than *those* precautionary measures of Indian morality. The third edict, for example (Avadana-Sastra I), "concerning unclean potherbs," ordains that the sole food allowed to the Chandalas shall be garlic and onions, considering that the holy writings forbid giving them grain, grain-bearing fruits, *water*, and fire. The same edict ordains that the water they require must neither be taken out of rivers, springs, or ponds, but only out of the entrances to swamps, and out of holes made by the footsteps of animals. In the same manner they are forbidden both to wash their clothes and *to wash themselves*, since the water, which is conceded to them as a favour, must only be used to quench their thirst. Finally, there is a prohibition forbidding the Sudra women to assist the Chandala women at child-birth, in like manner also a prohibition forbidding the latter *to assist one another on such occasions* . . . —The result of such sanitary regulations did not fail to appear: deadly epidemics, frightful sexual diseases, and, in consequence thereof, the "law of the knife" once more, which ordained circumcision for the male children and the removal of the *labia minora* in the females.—Manu himself says: "The Chandalas are the fruit of adultery, incest, and crime (this is the *necessary* consequence of the concept of breeding). They shall only have the rags of corpses for clothing, for vessels they shall only have broken pottery, for ornaments old iron, for the worship of God only the evil spirits; they shall wander from place to place without repose. They are forbidden to write from left to right, or to use the right hand in writing: the use of the right hand and from left-to-right are reserved exclusively for the *virtuous*, for persons of *race*."

4

These enactments are sufficiently instructive: here for once we have *Aryan* humanity, perfectly pure, perfectly original,—we learn that the idea of "pure blood" is the contrary of a harmless idea. On the other hand, it becomes manifest in *which* nation the hatred, the Chandala hatred against this "humanity," has immortalised itself, where it has become religion, and *genius* . . . From this point of view the Gospels are documents of the first importance, and the book of Enoch even more so. Christianity springing out of a Jewish root, and only comprehensible as a growth of this soil, represents the *movement counter* to every morality of breeding, of race, and of privilege: it is *anti-Aryan* religion *par excellence*: Christianity, the transvaluation of all Aryan values, the triumph of Chandala values, the gospel preached to the poor and lowly, the collective insurrection against "race" of all the downtrodden, the wretched, the ill-constituted, the misfortunate,—undying Chandala revenge as *religion of love* . . .

5

The morality of *breeding* and the morality of *taming* are perfectly worthy of one another as regards the expedients for achieving their ends: we may lay it down as our highest proposition, that in order to *create* morality, it is necessary to have the absolute will to the contrary. This is the great, the *unearthly* problem which I have longest applied myself to: the psychology of the "improvers" of mankind. A small and modest matter after all, so-called *pia fraus*, gave me the first access to this problem: *pia fraus*, the heritage of all philosophers and priests who have "improved" mankind. Neither Manu, nor Plato, nor Confucius, nor the Jewish and Christian teachers, have ever doubted of their *right* to use falsehood. They have not doubted *with regard to quite other rights* . . . Expressed in a formula one might say that *all* the measures hitherto used for the purpose of moralising mankind, have been fundamentally *immoral.* —

WHAT THE GERMANS LACK

1

Among Germans at present, it is not sufficient to have *esprit*; one must appropriate it practically, one must presume to have it.

Perhaps I know the Germans, perhaps I may even say a few truths to them. Modern Germany exhibits a great amount of hereditary and indoctrinated capacity, so that it can even spend prodigally for a while its accumulated treasure of force. It is *not* a high civilisation that has here gained the ascendency, still less a delicate taste, or a superior "beauty" of the instincts, but *manlier* virtues than any other country in Europe can exhibit. Much good humour and self-respect, much firmness in dealing with one another, in reciprocity of obligations, much laboriousness, much endurance,—and a hereditary moderation which requires the goad rather than the brake. I also add that here there is still obedience, without its being humiliating . . . And nobody despises his opponent . . .

It is obviously my wish to be just to the Germans: I should not like to be unfaithful to myself in this matter,—consequently I have to tell them what I object to. It costs dear to attain to power: power *stupefies* . . . The Germans—they were once called the nation of thinkers; do they really at present think at all?—The Germans are bored with intellect now-a-days, they mistrust it, politics swallow up all seriousness for really intellectual matters,—"*Deutschland, Deutschland über alles,*"[1] I fear that has been the end of German philosophy . . . "Are there German philosophers? are there German poets? are there *good* German books?" people ask me abroad: I blush; but with the courage which is peculiar to me even in desperate cases, I answer, "Yes, *Bismarck!*"—Could I even dare to confess what books people read now-a-days? . . . Accursed instinct of mediocrity!—

---

[1] The German national hymn.

2

—Who has not had melancholy reflections concerning the *possibilities* of German *esprit!* But this nation has arbitrarily stupefied itself for nearly a thousand years: nowhere have the two great European narcotics, alcohol and Christianity, been more wickedly misused. Recently, a third has been introduced, with which alone every refined and bold activity of intellect can be wiped out—music, our constipated, constipating German music.—How much moody heaviness, lameness, humidity, and dressing-gown mood, how much *beer* is in German intelligence! How is it really possible that young men, who consecrate their existence to the most intellectual ends, do not feel in themselves the first instinct of intellectuality, the *self-preservative instinct of intellect*—and drink beer? . . . The alcoholism of the learned youth is perhaps no interrogative sign with reference to their learnedness—one can be very learned even without *esprit*,—but in every other respect it remains a problem.—Where do we not find it, the mild intellectual degeneration caused by beer! I once laid my finger on an instance of such degeneration, a case almost become celebrated—that of our first German freethinker, the *shrewd* David Strauss, who degenerated into an author of a drinking-saloon gospel and a "New Belief." Not with impunity had he made his vow in verses to the "lovely brunette"[1]—loyalty to death . . .

3

—I spoke of German *esprit* to the effect that it becomes coarser and shallower. Is that enough? In reality, it is something quite different which frightens me; German seriousness, German profundity, and German *passion* in intellectual matters, are more and more on the decline. Pathos has altered, not merely intellectuality.—I come in contact now and then with German universities: what an atmosphere prevails among their scholars, what withered, contented, and lukewarm intellectuality! It would be a great misunderstanding if a person should adduce German science by way of objection to me, and, besides, it would be a proof that he had not read a word of my writings. For seventeen years I have not tired of showing the *intellectually enervating* influence of our modern scientific pursuits. The severe helotism to which the immense extent of the sciences at present condemns every individual, is a principal reason why the more fully, more richly, and *more profoundly* endowed natures no longer find suitable education and suitable *educators*. There is nothing from which our civilisation

---

[1]Beer

suffers *more* than from the superfluity of presumptuous hodmen and fragmental humanities; our universities are, against their will, the real forcing houses for this mode of stunted growth of intellectual instincts. And all Europe has already an idea of it—grand politics deceive nobody . . . Germany is more and more regarded as the *flat-land* of Europe.—I still *seek* for a German with whom *I* might be serious in my own way,—how much more for one with whom I could be cheerful! *Twilight of the Idols*: ah! who can conceive at present *from what seriousness* a philosopher here recruits himself! Our cheerfulness is what is least understood . . .

4

Let us make an estimate. It is not only manifest that German civilisation declines, there is also sufficient reason for it. No one can ultimately spend more than he possesses:—that is true of individuals, it is true also of nations. If we expend our means on power, grand politics, economy, international commerce, parliamentarism, or military interests,—if we give away the quantity of understanding, seriousness, will, and self-overcoming, which constitutes us, on *this* side, it is lacking on the other. Civilisation and the state—let us not delude ourselves with regard to the matter—are antagonists: "civilised state" is merely a modern idea. The one lives on the other, the one flourishes at the expense of the other. All great periods of civilisation are periods of political *décadence*: whatever has been great as regards civilisation, has been non-political, even *anti-political*.—Goethe's heart opened on the phenomenon of Napoléon,—it closed on the "War of Liberation" . . . At the same time that Germany comes forward as a great power, France acquires a changed importance as a power of civilisation. Much new intellectual seriousness and passion is already transferred to Paris; the question of pessimism, for example; the question of Wagner, and almost all psychological and artistic questions are there discussed in an incomparably more refined and more thorough manner than in Germany,—the Germans themselves are *incapacitated* for that kind of seriousness.—In the history of European civilisation there is one thing especially which the rise of the "Empire" indicates: a *displacement of the centre of gravity*. Everybody is aware of it already: in the most important matter—and that is civilisation—the Germans are no longer of any account. It is asked: have you even a single intellect to point to that counts in Europe, as your Goethe, your Hegel, your Heinrich Heine, and your Schopenhauer counted?—There is no end of astonishment that there is no longer a single German philosopher.—

5

In all higher education in Germany, the main thing has been lost: the *end*, as well as the *means* for reaching it. That education, *culture*, itself, is the end—and *not* "the Empire;" that for this end there is need of *educators*—*not* public-school teachers and university scholars: that has been forgotten . . . Educators are necessary, *who are themselves educated*—superior, noble intellects, who are proved every moment, who are proved whether they speak or are silent, mature and *sweetened* civilisations,—*not* the learned lubbers which the public-school and universities at present offer to the youths as "higher nurses." The educators *are lacking* (save the exceptions of exceptions)—the *primary* pre-requisite of education: hence the *décadence* of German civilisation.—One of those rarest exceptions is my worthy friend, Jacob Burckhardt of Bâle: it is to him, above all, that Bâle owes its pre-eminence in Humanity.—What the "higher schools" of Germany actually realise, is a brutal training in order that, with the least possible loss of time, an immense number of young men may be fitted to be used, *used up*, as government officials. "Higher education" and *immense numbers*—that is a contradiction in principle. All higher education belongs to the exceptions only: one has to be privileged to have a right to so high a privilege. All that is great, all that is fine, can never be a common possession: *pulchrum est paucorum hominum.*—What *determines* the *décadence* of German civilisation? That "higher education" is no longer a *privilege*—democratism of "universal," *communised* "culture" . . . Not to forget that military privileges compel the *too-great-attendance* at the higher schools, which means their ruin.—In the Germany of to-day no one is any longer at liberty to give his children a noble education: our "higher" schools are all of them adapted to the most equivocal mediocrity, as regards their teachers, plans of study, and educational aims. And everywhere there is an unbecoming haste, as if something were wrong, when the young man of twenty-three is not yet "finished," does not yet know the answer to the "main question:" *what* calling?—A higher class of men, let it be said, do not like "callings," precisely because they know they are called . . . They have time, they take their time, they do not at all think about getting "finished;"—at thirty years of age a person is a beginner, a child in the sphere of high civilisation.—Our over-filled public-schools, our overloaded, stupefied public-school teachers are a scandal: there may perhaps be *motives* for defending this condition of things, as the professors of Heidelberg have done recently,—there are no reasons for it.

6

In order not to come short of my special mode (which is *affirmative*, and only deals mediately and involuntarily with contradiction and criticism), I at once state the three tasks for the fulfilment of which educators are required. The youth have to learn to *see*, they have to learn to *think*, they have to learn to *speak* and *write*: the object in all three cases is a noble civilisation. — To learn to *see* — to accustom the eye to quietness, to patience, to reserve; to postpone judgment, to survey and comprehend each case from all sides. This is the *first* preliminary schooling for intellectuality: *not* to react immediately upon a stimulus, but to get the checking, the settling instincts in hand. Learning to *see*, as I understand it, is almost the same thing as in unphilosophical language is called strong will: the essential thing there is just *not* to "will," — the *ability* to defer decision. All spiritlessness, all vulgarity rests on the inability to offer resistance to a stimulus — people are *obliged* to react, they follow every impulse. In many cases such a compulsion is already morbidness, *décadence*, a symptom of exhaustion, — almost all that unphilosophical crudeness designates by the word "vice," is merely that physiological inability *not* to react. — A practical application of having learned to see: — As *learners*, people will in general have become slow, mistrustful, and reluctant. With hostile quietude they will let the strange and the *new* of every description approach at first, — they will withdraw their hand, so as not to be touched by it. The being open by all doors, the servile prostration before every insignificant fact, the continuous lurking to put one's self, to *throw* one's self among other people and other things, in short, vaunted modern "objectivity" is bad taste, it is *ignoble par excellence*. —

7

Learning *to think*: people have no longer any notion of it in our schools. Even in the universities, even among philosophical scholars themselves, logic begins to die out, alike as a theory, as a practice, and as a *profession*. Let anyone read German books: there is no longer the remotest recollection that a technique, a plan of instruction, and a will to reach proficiency are required for thinking, — that thinking requires to be learned as dancing requires to be learned, as a mode of dancing . . . Who among the Germans as yet knows by experience that refined tremor which *nimble feet* in the field of intellect communicate to all muscles! — the stiff doltishness of intellectual bearing, the *clumsy* hand in grasping — that is German in such a degree that abroad it is altogether confounded with the German nature. The German has no fingers for *nuances* . . . That the Germans have even endured their philosophers, more especially that most deformed conceptual cripple that has ever existed, the *great* Kant, gives no small concept of German elegance. — In effect, no form of *dancing* can be excluded from a *high-class education* — ability to dance with the feet, with concepts, and with words: have I still to say one must be capable of it with the *pen* also — one must learn to *write?* — But at this point I should become a perfect puzzle to German readers . . .

ROVING EXPEDITIONS
OF AN INOPPORTUNE PHILOSOPHER

1

My impracticables.—Seneca, or the toreador of virtue.

Rousseau, or return to nature *in impuris naturalibus.*

Schiller, or the moral Trumpeter of Säckingen.—*Dante,* or the hyena *poetising* in tombs.—*Kant,* or *cant* as an intelligible character.—*Victor Hugo,* or Pharos in the sea of absurdity.—*Liszt,* or the school of running—after women.—*George Sand,* or *lactea ubertas; i.e.* the milk-cow with "the fine style."—*Michelet,* or enthusiasm which strips off the coat . . . *Carlyle,* or pessimism as an undigested dinner.—*John Stuart Mill,* or offensive transparency.—*Les frères de Goncourt,* or the two Ajaxes struggling with Homer. Music by Offenbach.—*Zola,* or "the delight to stink."

2

Renan.—Divinity, or the perversion of reason by "original sin" (Christianity): witness Renan, who, whenever he ventures a more general affirmation or negation, fails to catch the point with painful regularity. For example, he would like to unite into one *la science* and *la noblesse; la science,* however, belongs to democracy—that is perfectly obvious. He desires, with no little ambition, to represent an intellectual aristocratism; but at the same time he lies on his knees (and not on his knees only) before the anti-thetical doctrine, the *évangile des humbles* . . . What is the good of all freethinking, modernism, gibing, and wry-necked dexterity, if you continue to be a Christian, a Roman Catholic, and even a priest, in your intestines! Renan's ingenuity lies in his seductiveness, just as in the case of the Jesuit and the confessor; the broad priestly smirk is not lacking in his intellectuality,—like all priests he only becomes dangerous when he loves. Nobody equals him in his faculty for idolising in a fatally dangerous manner . . . This spirit of Renan, a spirit which *enervates,* is an *additional* calamity for poor, sick, feeble-willed France.

3

Sainte-Beuve.—Nothing of a man; fully of petty resentment against all masculine intellects. Wanders about delicate, curious, tired, "pumping" people,—a female after all, with a woman's revengefulness and a woman's sensuousness. As a psychologist a genius for *médisance*; inexhaustibly rich in expedients for the purpose; nobody understands better how to mix poison with praise. Plebeian in his lowest instincts and allied with the *ressentiment* of Rousseau: *consequently* a Romanticist— for Rousseau's instinct grunts and yearns for revenge under all *romantisme*. A revolutionist, though held tolerably in check by fear. Ill at ease in presence of everything possessing strength (public opinion, the Academy, the Court, and even Port Royal). Embittered against all greatness in men and things, against all that believes in itself. Poet enough and half-woman enough to be sensible of greatness as a power; continually turning like the celebrated worm, because he continually feels himself trodden upon. As a critic, without a standard, without firmness, and without backbone, with the tongue of the cosmopolitan *libertin* in favour of variety, but even without sufficient courage to confess the *libertinage*. As an historian, without a philosophy, without the *power* of philosophic vision,—on that account declining the task of passing judgment in all great questions, holding up "objectivity" as a mask. He behaves otherwise, however, with regard to all matters where a delicate, worn-out taste is the highest tribunal; there he really has the courage of himself, pleasure in himself—there he is a *master.*—In some respects a prototype of Baudelaire.—

4

The *Imitatio Christi* is one of the books which I cannot hold in my hand without a physiological resistance: it exhales a *parfum* of the eternally feminine, for which one has to be French—or Wagnerian . . . This saint has such a way of speaking about love that even the Parisiennes become curious.—I am told that A. Comte, that *shrewdest* of Jesuits, who wanted to lead his fellow countrymen to Rome by the *indirect route* of science, inspired himself by this book. I believe it: the "religion of the heart" . . .

5

G. Eliot.—They have got rid of Christian God, and now think themselves obliged to cling firmer than ever to Christian morality: that is *English* consistency; we shall not lay the blame of it on ethical girls à la Eliot. In England for every little emancipation from divinity, people have to re-acquire respectability by becoming moral fanatics in an awe-inspiring manner. That is the *penalty* they have to pay there.—With us it is different. When we give up Christian belief, we thereby deprive ourselves of the *right* to maintain a stand on Christian morality. This is *not* at all obvious of itself; we have again and again to make this point clear, in defiance of English shallow-pates. Christianity is a system, a view of things, consistently thought out and *complete*. If we break out of it a fundamental idea, the belief in God, we thereby break the whole into pieces: we have no longer anything determined in our grasp. Christianity presupposes that man does not know, *cannot* know what is good for him and what is evil; he believes in God, who alone knows. Christian morality is a command, its origin is transcendent, it is beyond all criticism, beyond all right of criticism; it has solely truth, if God is truth,—it stands or falls with the belief in God.—If in fact the English imagine they know, of their own accord, "intuitively" what is good and evil, if they consequently imagine they have no more need of Christianity as a guarantee of morality; that itself is merely the *result* of the ascendency of Christian valuation, and an expression of its *strength* and *profundity*: to such extent that the origin of English morality has been forgotten: to such an extent that the strictly conditional character of its right to existence is no longer perceived. Morality is not as yet a problem for the English . . .

6

George Sand.—I read the first "Letters d'un Voyageur:" like all derived from Rousseau, false, artificial, inflated, exaggerated. I cannot stand this variegated wall paper style; nor the vulgar ambition for generous feelings. But the worst, surely, is the woman's coquetry with masculine characteristics, with the manners of ill-bred boys.—How cold she must have been withal, this insufferable artist! She wound herself up like a timepiece—and wrote . . . Cold like Hugo, like Balzac, like all Romanticists, as soon as they began to write! And how self-complacently she may then have reposed, this productive writing cow, who, like her master Rousseau himself, had in her something German in the bad sense, and at all events, was only possible owing to the decline of French taste!—But Renan adores her . . .

7

A moral for psychologists.—Never to occupy one's self with colportage psychology! Never to observe for the sake of observing! That results in false optics, in squinting, in something forced and exaggerated. Experiencing, as a *desire* to experience—that does not do. In expericncing anything, one *must* not look towards one's self; every look then becomes an "evil eye." A born psychologist is instinctively on his guard against seeing for the sake of seeing; the same is true of the born painter. He never works "according to nature,"—he leaves the sifting and expressing of the "case," of "nature," or of the "experienced," to his instinct, to his *camera obscura* . . . He only becomes conscious of what is *general*, the conclusion, the result; he is unacquainted with that arbitrary abstracting from single cases.—What is the result when people do otherwise? for example, when they carry on colportage psychology after the manner of great and small Parisian *romanciers*? *That* mode of business lies in wait, as it were, for the actual, it brings home a handful of curiosities every evening . . . But let us only see what finally results from it.—A pile of daubs, at the best a mosaic, in every case, something pieced together, disquieting, loud-coloured. The Goncourts are the worst sinners in this respect; they do not put three sentences together, which are not simply painful to the eye, to the *psychologist*-eye.— Nature, estimated artistically, is no model. It exaggerates, it distorts, it leaves gaps. Nature is *accident*. Studying "according to nature" seems to me a bad sign; it betrays subjection, weakness, fatalism; this lying-in-the-dust before *petits faits* is unworthy of a *complete* artist. Seeing *what is*—that belongs to another species of intellects, to the *anti-artistic*, to the practical. One has to know *who* one is . . .

8

A *psychology of the artist*.—To the existence of art, to the existence of any æsthetic activity or perception whatsoever, a preliminary psychological condition is indispensable, namely, *ecstasy*. Ecstasy must first have intensified the sensitiveness of the whole mechanism; until this takes place art is not realised. All kinds of ecstasy, however differently conditioned, possess this power; above all the ecstasy of sexual excitement, the oldest and most primitive form of ecstasy. In like manner the ecstasy which follows in the train of all great desires, of all strong emotions; the ecstasy of the feast, of the contest, of a daring deed, of victory, of all extreme agitation; the ecstasy of cruelty; the ecstasy in destruction; the ecstasy under certain meteorological influences—for example, spring ecstasy; or under the influence of narcotics; finally, the ecstasy of will, the ecstasy of an overcharged and surging will.—The essential thing in ecstasy is the feeling of increased power and profusion. Out of this feeling we impart to things, we *constrain* them to accept something from us, we force them by violence;—this proceeding is called *idealising*. Let us here free ourselves from a prejudice: idealising does *not* consist, as is commonly believed, in an abstraction or deduction of the insignificant or the contingent. An immense *forcing out* of principal traits is rather the decisive characteristic, so that the others thereby disappear.

9

In this condition we enrich everything out of our own profusion; what we see, and what we wish for we see enlarged, crowded, strong, and overladen with power. He who, in this condition, transforms things till they mirror his power,—till they are reflections of his perfection. This *constraint* to transform into the perfect is—art. Everything that he is not, nevertheless becomes for him a delight in himself; in art man enjoys himself as perfection.—It would be allowable to imagine an opposite state of things, a specific anti-artisticalness of instinct—a mode of being which would impoverish everything, attenuate everything, make everything consumptive. In fact, history furnishes us with abundance of such anti-artists, persons with starved lives, who must necessarily lay hold of things, drain them, and make them *more emaciated*. This is the case with the genuine Christian, Pascal, for example; a Christian, who is at the same time an artist, *is not to be found*. Let no one be childish enough to refer me to the case of Raphael, or to any homœopathic Christian of the nineteenth century. Raphael said yea, he did yea; consequently Raphael was no Christian . . .

10

What do the antithetical notions *Apollinian* and *Dionysian* (which I have introduced into æsthetics) imply, when we conceive of them both as modes of ecstasy? Apollinian ecstasy above all keeps the eye on the alert so that it acquires the faculty of vision. The painter, the sculptor, and the epic poet, are visionaries *par excellence*. In the Dionysian condition, on the other hand, the entire emotional system is excited, and has its energies augmented; so that it discharges itself simultaneously by all channels of expression, and forces the faculties of representation, of imitation, of transfiguration, of metamorphosis—all kinds of mimicry and acting—into activity at one and the same time. The essential thing is the easiness of the metamorphosis, the *incapacity* to resist a stimulus (similar to the case of certain hysterical patients, who also act *every* rôle at every hint). It is impossible for Dionysian man not to understand any suggestion, he overlooks no symptom of emotion, he possesses the highest manifestation of knowing and divining instinct, as also the highest development of communicative art. He assumes every external appearance, every emotion; he changes himself continually.—Music, as we understand it at present, is also a collective excitement and collective discharge of the emotions, nevertheless it is only the survival of a much wider world of emotional expression, a mere *residuum* of Dionysian histrionism. To make music possible as a separate art, several of the senses—especially muscular sense—have here been eliminated (relatively at least, for to a certain extent all rhythm still speaks to our muscles); so that man no longer immediately imitates and gives bodily expression to every feeling. Nevertheless *that* is the Dionysian normal condition, at any rate the original condition: music is the slowly attained specialisation of this condition at the cost of the faculties nearest akin to it.

11

The actor, the mime, the dancer, the musician, and the lyric poet are fundamentally akin in their instincts and one in their essence, but they have gradually specialised and separated from one another—till indeed they are in contradiction. The lyric poet remained longest united with the musician; the actor remained longest connected with the dancer.— The *architect* represents neither a Dionysian, nor an Apollinian condition; here it is the great act of will, the will which removes mountains, ecstasy of strong will that is desirous of art. The most powerful men have always inspired architects; the architect has always been under the suggestion of power. In the work of architecture pride, triumph over gravity and will to power, are intended to display themselves; architecture is a sort of eloquence of power embodied in forms, sometimes persuading, even flattering, and sometimes merely commanding. The highest feeling of power and security is expressed in that which has the *grand style*. Power which needs no further demonstration, which scorns to please, which answers unwillingly, which has no sense of any witness near it, which is without consciousness that there is opposition to it, which reposes in *itself*, fatalistic, a law among laws: *that* is what speaks of itself as the grand style.

12

I read the "Life of Thomas Carlyle," that unconscious and unintended *farce*, that heroico-moral interpretation of dyspeptic conditions.— Carlyle, a man of strong words and attitudes, a rhetorician from *necessity*, who was continually irritated by the longing for a strong belief *and* the feeling of incapacity for it (in that respect a typical Romanticist!). The longing for a strong belief is *not* evidence of a strong belief, rather the contrary. *When one has this belief*, one may allow one's self the choice luxury of scepticism; one is sufficiently sure, sufficiently resolute, and sufficiently bound for doing so. Carlyle deafens something in his nature by the *fortissimo* of his reverence for men of strong belief, and by his rage against the less stupid; he *requires* noise. A constant, passionate *insincerity* towards himself—that is his *proprium;* he is interesting, and will remain interesting thereby. In England, to be sure, he is admired precisely on account of his sincerity . . . Well, that is English; and in consideration that the English are the people of consummate *cant,* it is not merely conceivable, but appropriate. After all, Carlyle is an English atheist, who aspires to honour for *not* being one.

13

Emerson.—Much more enlightened, more discursive, more varied, more refined than Carlyle, above all more fortunate . . . One who instinctively nourishes himself solely with ambrosia, leaving alone what is indigestible in things. A man of taste in comparison with Carlyle.— Carlyle, who had much love for Emerson, said nevertheless, "He does not give *us* enough to chew," which may rightly be said, but not to Emerson's prejudice.—Emerson possesses that kind-hearted and ingenuous cheerfulness, which discourages all sternness; he does not by any means know how old he is already, and how young he will yet be;—he could say of himself, with an expression of Lope de Vega: "*yo me sucedo a mi mismo.*" His mind always finds reasons for being contented, and even grateful; and now and then verges on the cheerful transcendence of that worthy man, who, returning from a love appointment, *tanquam re bene gesta,* said thankfully, "*Ut desint vires, tamen est laudanda voluptas.*" —

14

Anti-Darwin.—As regards the celebrated "struggle for life," it seems to me, in the meantime, to be more asserted than proved. It occurs, but only as an exception; the general aspect of life is *not* a state of want or hunger; it is rather a state of opulence, luxuriance, and even absurd prodigality,—where there is a struggle, it is a struggle for *power.*—We must not confound Malthus with nature. Granted, however, that this struggle exists—and in fact it does occur—its results, alas, are the reverse of what the Darwinian school wish, the reverse of what one *might* perhaps wish, in accordance with them: it is prejudicial to the strong, the privileged, the fortunate exceptions. The species does *not* grow in perfection: the weak again and again get the upper hand of the strong,—their large number, and their *greater cunning* are the cause of it. Darwin forgot the intellect (that was English!); *the weak have more intellect* . . . One must need intellect in order to acquire it; one loses it when it is no longer necessary. He who was strength rids himself of intellect ("let it go hence!"[1] is what people think in Germany at present, "the *Empire* will remain" . . .). As is obvious, under intellect I comprehend foresight, patience, craft, dissimulation, grand self-control, and all modifications of *mimicry*. A great deal of so-called virtue is included under mimicry.

15

Psychologist casuistry. — This individual is an expert in the knowledge of men: for what end is he actually studying men? He wants to get some little advantages over them, or even some great advantages, — he is a *politicus!* . . . That individual is also an expert in the knowledge of men, and you say he wants nothing for himself thereby, he is one of the grand "impersonal." Look at him more carefully! Perhaps he even wants a *more reprehensible* advantage: to feel himself superior to men, to be allowed to look down on them, not to confound himself with them any longer. This "impersonal one" is a *despiser* of men; the former is the more humane species, whatever appearance may indicate. He at least places himself on an equality with men, he places himself *among* them . . .

16

The *psychological tact* of the Germans seems to me to be called in question by a whole series of cases, a list of which my modesty prevents me from bringing forward. In one case a remarkable inducement will not be lacking to establish my thesis: I have a grudge against the Germans for having made a mistake about *Kant* and his "back-door philosophy," as I call it, — that was *not* the type of intellectual honesty. — That other thing which I do not like to hear is a notorious "and:" the Germans say "Goethe *and* Schiller;" I am afraid lest they say "Schiller and Goethe" . . . Is this Schiller not yet *known?* — There are still worse "ands;" I have heard with my own ears, "Schopenhauer *and* Hartmann;" to be sure, only among university professors . . .

17

The most intellectual men, provided they are the most courageous, experience by far the most painful tragedies; but they reverence life just on that account, because it places its most powerful hostile forces in opposition to them.

---

[1]An allusion to Luther's song, Eine feste Burg ist unser Gott!

18

"Intellectual conscience." — Nothing seems to me to be rarer at present than genuine hypocrisy. I have a strong suspicion that the mild air of our civilisation is not beneficial to this plant. Hypocrisy belongs to the ages of strong belief when people did not part with their own belief, even under the *constraint* of showing off another belief. At present people part with it; or, what is more common, they provide themselves with a second belief, — in all cases they remain *honest*. Undoubtedly, there is at present a very much greater variety of convictions possible than there was formerly: possible, that is to say they are permitted, they do no *harm*. Out of this state of things tolerance towards one's self originates. — Tolerance towards one's self permits of several convictions; these live together in agreement, — they take care, as everybody does at present, not to compromise themselves. What does one compromise one's self with at present? If one is consistent. If one goes in a straight line. If one is less than quinquivocal. If one is genuine . . . I very much fear that modern man is simply too comfortable for some vices; so that these die out altogether. Everything wicked which is determined by strong will — perhaps there is nothing wicked without strength of will — degenerates to virtue in our lukewarm atmosphere . . . The few hypocrites I have become acquainted with, imitated hypocrisy; they were actors, like almost every tenth man at present. —

19

Beautiful and ugly. — Nothing is more conditioned, let us say more *restricted*, than our sense of the beautiful. A person who would try to think of it as detached from the delight of man in man would immediately lose his footing. The "beautiful in itself" is merely an expression, not even a concept. In the beautiful, man posits himself as the standard of perfection; in select cases he worships himself in that standard. A species *cannot* possibly do otherwise than thus to say yea to itself. Its *lowest* instinct, that of self-maintenance and self-expansion, still radiates in such sublimities. Man believes the world itself to be overcharged with beauty, — he *forgets* that he is the cause of it. He alone has endowed it with beauty, alas! only with very human, all-too-human beauty . . . In reality man mirrors himself in things; he counts everything beautiful which reflects his likeness; the verdict "beautiful" is man's *conceit of his species*. A little suspicion may in fact whisper the question into a sceptic's ear — Is the world really beautified, just because man thinks it is? Man has *humanised* it; that is all. But nothing, nothing whatever warrants us in supposing that it is just man who furnishes the model of the beautiful. Who knows how he appears in the eyes of a higher judge of taste? Perhaps risky? perhaps even entertaining? perhaps a little arbitrary? . . . "Oh divine Dionysos, why dost thou pull mine ears?" asked Ariadne once of her philosophic lover, in one of the celebrated dialogues at Naxos. "I find a sort of humour in thine ears, Ariadne: why are they not longer?"

20

Nothing is beautiful, except man: all æsthetics rest on this *naïveté*, it is their *first* truth. Let us straightway add the second: nothing is ugly, except *degenerating* man;—the domain of æsthetic judgment is thereby limited.—Re-examined physiologically, all that is ugly weakens and afflicts man. It reminds him of deterioration, of danger, and of impotence; he actually suffers loss of power by it. The effect of ugliness can be measured by the dynamometer. Whenever man is depressed he has a sense of the proximity of something "ugly." His sense of power, his will to power, his courage, his pride—they decrease with the ugly, they increase with the beautiful. In both cases *we draw an inference*, the premises of which are accumulated in enormous fulness in instinct. The ugly is understood as a sign and symptom of degeneration; that which reminds us in the remotest manner of degeneracy prompts us to pronounce the verdict, "ugly." Every indication of exhaustion, gravity, age, or lassitude; every kind of constraint, such as cramp or paralysis; and above all the odour, the colour, and the likeness of decomposition or putrefaction, be it utterly attenuated even to a symbol:—all these things call forth a similar reaction, the evaluation "ugly." A *hatred* is there excited: whom does man hate there? There can be no doubt: the *decline of his type*. The hatred is inspired by the most profound instinct of the species; there is horror, foresight, profundity, and far-reaching vision in it—it is the profoundest of all hatreds. On account of it, art is *profound*.

21

Schopenhauer.—Schopenhauer, the last German who comes into consideration (who is a *European* event, like Goethe, like Hegel, like Heinrich Heine, and *not merely* a local, a "national" occurrence), is a case of the first rank for a psychologist, as being an ill-natured, ingenious attempt to bring into the field, in favour of a general nihilistic valuation of the whole of life, the very opposite instances, the grand self-affirmations of "will to life," the exuberant forms of life. He has interpreted in turn, *art*, heroism, genius, beauty, grand sympathy, knowledge, will for truth, and tragedy, as phenomena resulting from "negation," or from the need of negation of "will,"—the most spurious psychological mintage, Christianity excepted, which history records. Looked at more closely, he appears therein merely the heir of Christian interpretation: only, he knew how to *justify* in a Christian sense (*i.e.* in a nihilistic sense) even the great facts of human civilisation, which had been *repudiated* by Christianity,—interpreting them as ways leading to "salvation," as early forms of "salvation," as *stimulantia* for making "salvation" requisite . . .

22

I take a single instance. Schopenhauer speaks of *beauty* with melancholy ardour: what is his ultimate reason for it? Because he sees in it a *bridge* by which one may get further on, or acquire an incentive to get further on . . . He regards it as a momentary salvation from "will"—it allures to everlasting salvation . . . He especially praises it as the Saviour from the "focus of will," from sexuality,—in beauty he sees the generative impulse *negatived* . . . Strange saint! Somebody contradicts thee, I fear it is nature. *For what end* at all is there beauty of tone, colour, odour, and rhythmical motion in nature? What *evolves the display* of beauty? Fortunately a philosopher contradicts him also: no less an authority than divine Plato (Schopenhauer himself calls him divine) maintains another thesis: that all beauty incites to procreation,—that this is precisely the *proprium* of its operation, from its most sensuous, up to its most intellectual manifestations . . .

23

Plato goes further. He says, with an innocence for which one must be Greek and not "Christian," that there would be no Platonic philosophy at all, were there not such handsome youths in Athens; it was only the sight of them which put the soul of the philosopher into an erotic ecstasy, and gave it no rest until it had implanted the seed of all high things in such a fine soil. A strange saint also!—one does not trust one's ears, even if one trusts Plato. At least, one surmises that they philosophised *differently* at Athens, above all that they philosophised publicly. Nothing is less Grecian than the conceptual cobweb spinning of a recluse, *amor intellectualis dei*, according to the mode of Spinoza. Philosophy, according to Plato's mode, could rather be defined as an erotic competition, as a further development and an inwardising of the old agonistic system of gymnastics, with its *pre-requisites* . . . What ultimately grew out of this philosophical erotic of Plato? A new technical form of Grecian *agon*, dialectics.—I further call to mind, *in opposition to* Schopenhauer and to the honour of Plato, that the whole of the higher civilisation and literature of classical France has also grown up on the soil of sexual interest. One may search everywhere in it for gallantry, sensuality, erotic competition, "woman," — one will never search in vain . . .

24

L'art pour l'art. — The fighting against the end in art is always warfare against the *moralising* tendency in art, against its subordination to morality. *L'art pour l'art*: that is, "the devil take morality." But this very hostility betrays the domination of the prejudice. When the end of the ethical preacher and improver of mankind has been excluded from art, it does not at all follow that art in itself is without an end, without a goal, meaningless; in short, *l'art pour l'art* — a serpent which bites its own tail. "No end at all, rather than a moral end!" — thus speaks pure passion. A psychologist, on the other hand, asks, what does all art do? does it not praise? does it not glorify? does it not select? does it not bring into prominence? In each of these cases it *strengthens or weakens* certain valuations . . . Is this only a contingent matter? an accident? something with which the instinct of the artist would not at all be concerned? Or rather, is it not the pre-requisite which *enables* the artist to do something? Is his fundamental instinct directed towards art? or is it not rather directed towards the sense of art, namely, *life?* towards a *desirableness of life?* — Art is the great stimulus to life, how could art be understood as purposeless, as aimless, as *l'art pour l'art?* — A question still remains: art makes manifest also much that is ugly, harsh, and questionable in life, — does it not thereby seem to make life intolerable? — In fact there have been philosophers who gave this meaning to it: Schopenhauer taught that the whole purpose of art is "to disengage from will;" he honoured it as the great usefulness of tragedy "to dispose to resignation." — This however — I have already hinted at it — is pessimistic optics and the "evil eye:" — one must appeal to artists themselves. *What of his own personality does the artist communicate to others in tragedy?* It is not precisely the fearless state of mind in presence of the frightful and the questionable which he exhibits? — This state of mind is highly desirable in itself; whoever knows it, honours it with the highest regard. He communicates it, he *is obliged* to communicate it, provided he is an artist, a genius of communication. Bravery and self-possession in presence of a powerful enemy, an awful calamity, or a problem which awakens dread — it is this *triumphal* condition which the tragic artist selects and glorifies. In presence of tragedy the martial spirit in us celebrates its Saturnalia; he who is accustomed to

affliction, he who seeks affliction—*heroic* man—extols his existence with tragedy,—to him alone the tragic artist offers the
draught of this sweetest cruelty.—

25

To put up with men, to keep open house with one's heart: that is liberal—but it is merely liberal. We recognise the hearts which are capable of *noble* hospitality by the many curtained windows and closed
shutters: they keep their best rooms vacant. Why is that?—Because they
expect guests with whom they have *not* to "put up" . . .

26

We no longer estimate ourselves sufficiently, when we communicate
ourselves. Our true experiences are not at all loquacious. They could
not communicate themselves, even if they wished. The reason is that
they have no language. We have already got beyond what we can express
in words. In all speaking there is an inkling of contempt. Language, it
seems, has only been invented for the average, the middling, and the
communicative. With speech the speaker has already *vulgarised* himself.—Extract from Morals for deaf-mutes and other philosophers.

27

"This likeness is charmingly beautiful!"[1]—Literary woman, discontented, agitated, desolate in heart and bowels, ever listening with
painful curiosity to the imperative which whispers out of the depths of
her organisation, *"aut liberi aut libri;"* literary woman, cultured enough
to understand the voice of nature even when it speaks in Latin, and, on
the other hand, conceited enough and goose enough to speak secretly
with herself in French, *"je me verrai, je me lirai, je m'extasierai et je
dirai: Possible, que j'aie eu tant d'esprit?"* . . .

28

The "impersonal" speak.—"Nothing comes easier to us than to be wise,
patient, and superior. We drip with the oil of forbearance and sympathy, we are just to the verge of folly, we forgive all. For that very reason
we should keep ourselves somewhat more strictly disciplined; for that
very reason we should *cultivate* in ourselves from time to time a little
emotion, a little emotional vice. It may be hard for us, and among ourselves, we perhaps laugh at the appearance we thus present. But what

---

[1] Quotation from Mozart's opera, *The Magic Flute* (Aria of Tamino).

does it matter! There is no other method available for conquering our-selves; this is *our* asceticism, *our* penance" . . . *To become personal*—the virtue of the "impersonal" . . .

29

From a doctor's examination.—"What is the task of all higher instruc-tion?"—To make man a machine.—"What is the means?"—He has to learn to be tired.—"How is that attained?"—By the notion of duty.—"Who is his model here?"—The philologist: he teaches how to *fag.*—"Who is the perfect man?"—The government official.—"What philos-ophy gives the best formula for the government official?"—Kant's: the government official as thing in itself, appointed arbiter over the gov-ernment official as phenomenon.

30

The right to stupidity.—The fatigued and slow-breathing working man who looks good-humoured and lets things take their course, this typical figure whom one meets with in all classes of society in this age of labour (and of the "Empire!"—), quite claims *art* for himself in the present day, including the book, and above all the journal,—how much more beautiful nature, Italy. The man of the evening, with the "wild impulses lulled to sleep," of which Faust speaks, requires the health re-sort, the sea coast, the glaciers, Bayreuth . . . In such ages, art has a right to *pure folly*, as a sort of vacation-time for intellect, wit, and humour. That is what Wagner understood. *Pure folly* is a restorative . . .

31

Another problem of regimen.—The expedients with which Julius Cæsar protected himself from sickness and headache—prodigious marches, the simplest mode of life, uninterrupted living in the open air, and con-stant military exercise—are, on the whole, the measures for mainte-nance and protection from extreme liability to injury of that complex machine working under the highest pressure and called genius.

32

The immoralist speaks.—There is nothing *more* distasteful to a philoso-pher than man *in as far as he wishes.* When the philosopher sees man only in his doings, when he sees this bravest, most artful, and most en-during animal, led astray even into labyrinthine states of trouble, how worthy of admiration does man appear to him! The philosopher even furnishes man with encouragement . . . But he despises wishing man, "desirable" man also—and in general all desirabilities, all human *ideals*. If it were possible, a philosopher would be a nihilist, because he finds nothingness behind all human ideals. Or not even nothingness,—but only vileness, absurdity, sickness, cowardice, and fatigue: all sorts of dregs out of the *drained* goblet of his own life . . . Man, who, as a reality, is so worthy of reverence, how is it that he deserves no respect in as far as he manifests his wishes? Has he to do penance for being so accomplished as a reality? Has he to compensate for his activity, for the exertion of thought and will in every activity, by the stretching of his limbs in the imaginary and absurd? The history of his desirabilities has hitherto been the *partie honteuse* of man; one must be careful not to read too long in it. What justifies man is his reality,—it will for ever justify him. How much more worthy is actual man, compared with any merely wished, dreamt, or shamelessly failsified man! compared with any *ideal* man whatsoever . . . It is only ideal man that is distasteful to the philosopher.

33

Natural value of egotism.—Selfishness has as much value as the physiological value of him who possesses it: it may be very valuable, or it may be vile and contemptible. Each individual may be looked at with respect to whether he represents an ascending or a descending line of life. When that is determined, we have a canon for determining the value of his selfishness. If he represent the ascent of the line of life, his value is in fact very great—and on account of the collective life which in him makes a *further* step, the concern about his maintenance, about providing his *optimum* of conditions, may even be extreme. For the single person, the "individual," as hitherto understood both popularly and philosophically, is certainly an error: he is nothing "by himself," no atom, no "ring of the chain," nothing merely inherited from former times,—he is the embodiment of the one entire line of descent up to himself . . . If he represent descending development, decay, chronic degeneration, or sickening (diseases, taken on the whole, are phenomena which result from decay already present, they are *not* the causes of it), he has little worth, and the greatest fairness would have him *take away* as little as possible from the well-constituted. He is no more than their parasite then . . .

34

Christian and anarchist.—When the anarchist, as the mouth-piece of *degenerating* strata of society, demands "justice," "righteousness," and "equal rights" with embellished indignation, he is only under the influence of his lack of civilisation, which prevents him understanding *why* he is actually in trouble, — in *what respect* he is impoverished, that it is in vital vigour that he is impoverished . . . An impulse to seek for causes is strong in him: it must be somebody's fault that he is in a bad condition . . . Even "embellished indignation" itself is pleasant to him; it is an enjoyment for every poor devil to vilify, — it gives a taste of the ecstasy of power. Even lamenting and bewailing one's self can give life a charm by which it becomes tolerable. There is a refined dose of *revenge* in every lament; people reproach those who are different from them for their own bad condition, and under certain circumstances even for their wickedness, as if it were injustice, as if it involved *unpermitted* privilege. "If I be *canaille*, thou shouldst be so also:" it is on the basis of such logic that revolutions arise. — Bewailing one's self never does any good: it originates from weakness. Whether a person imputes his bad condition to others, or to *himself*—the socialist does the former, and the Christian, for example, does the latter—it makes no essential difference. That which both cases have in common, let us also say that which is *unworthy* in both cases, is that somebody is to be *blamed* for the suffering—in short, that the sufferer prescribes for himself the honey of revenge to alleviate his suffering. The objects towards which this need of revenge, as a need of *enjoyment,* is directed are furnished by occasional causes; the sufferer finds causes everywhere, which serve to cool his petty revenge, — if he is a Christian, we repeat, he finds the causes in *himself* . . . The Christian and the anarchist—both are *décadents.* — But moreover, when the Christian condemns, calumniates, and befouls the "*world,*" he does it from the same instinctive motive which impels the socialistic working man to condemn, calumniate, and befoul *society:* "doomsday" even is the delicious comfort of revenge, — revolution, the same as the socialistic working man expects, merely conceived as somewhat more remote. The "other world" itself—what would be the use of it, if it were not a means for befouling this world?

35

Criticism of décadence morality. —An "altruistic" morality, a morality which causes selfishness to *languish,* is, under all circumstances, a bad sign. This is true of the individual, it is especially true of peoples. The best is wanting, when selfishness begins to be deficient. To choose instinctively what is *self*-injurious, to be *allured* by "disinterested" motives, furnishes almost the formula for *décadence.* "Not to seek *one's own* advantage:" that is merely the moral fig-leaf for quite a different thing, for the physiological fact, — "one does not know any longer how

to *find* one's own advantage" . . . Disgregation of instincts!—It is at an
end with him when man becomes altruistic.—Instead of naïvely saying, "*I* am no longer of any account," the moral falsehood in the mouth
of the *décadent* says, "nothing is of any account,—*life* is of no account"
. . . Such an opinion is ultimately a great danger; it is contagious, soon
growing up luxuriantly to a tropical vegetation of ideas on the whole
morbid soil of society, at one time as a religion (Christianity), at another time as a philosophy (Schopenhauerity). Under certain circumstances such upas-tree vegetation, grown out of corruption, poisons *life*
with its far-reaching emanations for millenniums . . .

36

Morality for physicians.—The sick are parasites of society. In certain
conditions it is improper to live any longer. The continued vegetating
in cowardly dependence on physicians and prescriptions after the
meaning of life, the *right* to life, has been lost, should entail the profound contempt of society. The physicians, on the other hand, would
have to be agents for communicating this contempt,—not recipes for
their patients, but every day a new dose of *aversion* from them . . . To
create a new responsibility, the physician's responsibility, for all cases
where the highest interest of life, of *ascending* life, requires the re-
morseless crushing down and thrusting aside of *degenerating* life—for
example, for the right to procreation, for the right to be born, for the
right to live . . . To die proudly when it is no longer possible to live
proudly. Death selected voluntarily, death at the right time, consum-
mated with brightness and cheerfulness in the midst of children and
witnesses: so that an actual leave-taking is possible where *he is yet present* who takes his leave, as also an actual appraisement of what has been
realised and aspired after, a *summing up* of life—all in opposition to the
pitiable and horrifying comedy which Christianity has practised with
the hour of dying. We must never forgive Christianity for having taken
advantage of the weakness of the dying to outrage their consciences, for
having misused even the mode of death to arrive at valuations of men
and of the past. Here, in spite of all cowardice of prejudice, it is pri-
marily a question of re-establishing the correct evaluation, *i.e.* physiological evaluation, of so-called *natural* death,—which, in the end, is
nothing but an unnatural death, a suicide. One is never destroyed by
anyone but one's self. But natural death is a death under the most contemptible conditions, involuntary death, death at the *wrong* time, a
coward's death. Out of love to life we should desire a different kind of
death—voluntary, conscious, not accidental or by surprise . . . Finally,
an advice to Messrs. the pessimists and other *décadents*. We have not it

at our disposal to prevent being born; we can, however, rectify this error—for it is sometimes an error. When someone *does away with himself*, he does the noblest thing in the world; by so doing he has almost entitled himself to live . . . Society, what am I saying! *life* itself, is more advantaged thereby, than by any "life" of renunciation, anæmia, or other virtue,—one has freed others from one's presence, one has removed an *objection* to life . . . Pessimism, *pur, vert, only proves itself* by the self-refutation of Messrs. the pessimists: one must go a step further with one's logic, and not merely negative life with "Will and Representation," as Schopenhauer did, one must, *in the first place, negative Schopenhauer* . . . Pessimism, let us say in passing, notwithstanding its contagiousness, does not on the whole increase the infirmity of an age or race: it is the expression of infirmity. One succumbs to it as one succumbs to cholera; one has to be morbidly enough disposed for it. Pessimism itself does not make a single *additional décadent*; I call to mind the result of the statistics, that the years in which the cholera rages do not differ from the other years in the total number of deaths.

37

Whether we are become more moral.—As was to be expected, the whole *ferocity* of moral stupefaction, which avowedly passes for morality itself in Germany, has taken up arms against my conception, "beyond good and evil:" I could tell fine stories about it. My critics above all gave me the "undeniable superiority" of the moral sentiment of our age to reflect upon, the actual *progress* we have made in this respect; in comparison with *us*, a Cesare Borgia was on no account to be set up in my fashion as a "higher man," as a kind of *beyond-man*. A Swiss editor, of the "Bund," went so far (not without expressing his esteem of the courage for such a jeopardy) as to "understand" the meaning of my work to the effect that I proposed to do away with all decent sentiment. Very much obliged!—I permit myself, as an answer, to raise the question, *whether we are really become more moral*. That all the world believes it is already an objection against it . . . We modern men, very delicate, very readily injured, giving and taking consideration in a hundred ways, we conceit ourselves in fact that this delicate humanity which we manifest, this *realised* unanimity in forbearance, in helpfulness, and in mutual trust, is positive progress, and that we are thereby far above the men of the Renaissance. Every age, however, thinks in this manner, it *is obliged* to think thus. It is certain we could not place ourselves in Renaissance conditions; we could not even conceive ourselves placed in them: our nerves would not stand that reality, not to speak of our muscles. No progress, however, is demonstrated by this incapacity, but only a different, a later condition, weaker, tenderer, and more readily injured, out of which a *considerate* morality necessarily evolves. If we were to think of our tenderness and lateness, our physiological aging, as absent, our "humanising" morality also would forthwith lose its value (no morality has value in itself); it would even let us despise it. Let us not doubt, on the other hand, that we modern men, with our thick-wadded humanity, which will not by any means strike against a stone, would furnish a comedy to the contemporaries of Cesare Borgia to laugh themselves to death over. In fact we are extraordinarily amusing, though involuntarily, with our modern "virtues" . . . The decline of hostile and distrust-awakening instincts—for that would be our "progress"—represents only one of the consequences in the general decline of *vitality*: it costs a hundred times more pains and more foresight to effectuate an existence so conditioned and so late. Under such circumstances people mutually assist one another; to a certain extent everybody is sick, and everybody is a sick-nurse. That condition of things is then denominated "virtue:" among men who knew a different mode of life, fuller, more prodigal, more profuse, it would have had a different name, perhaps "cowardice," "pitiableness," or "old woman's morality" . . . Our softening of manners—that is my thesis, it is, if you will, my *innovation*—is a consequence of *décadence*; severity, frightfulness of manners may, inversely, be a consequence of superabundance of life: for then much can be dared, much can be challenged, and much also can be *squandered*. What was formerly a seasoning of life would be *poison* to us . . . To be indifferent—that also is a form of strength—for that likewise we are too old and too late: our morality of sympathy against which I was the first to give warning, that which one might designate as *l'impressionisme morale*, is a further expression of the physiological over-excitability possessed by all that is *décadent*. That movement which has attempted to introduce itself scientifically by means of Schopenhauer's *morality of sympathy*—a very unfortunate attempt!—is the true *décadence* movement in morals, and, as such, is intrinsically related to Christian morality. Vigorous eras, noble civilisations, see something contemptible in sympathy, in "brotherly love," in the lack of self-assertion and self-reliance.—Eras are to be measured by their *positive powers*: the period of the Renaissance accordingly, so profuse and fateful, presents itself as the last *great* period; and we modern men, with our anxious self-nursing and brotherly love, with our virtues of labour, unpretentiousness, fair play, and scientific spirit—accumulating, economic, mechanical,—we represent a *weak* period . . . Our virtues are determined, are *peremptorily called forth* by our weakness . . . "Equality," as an actual approximation to similarity, of which the theory of "equal rights" is but the expression, belongs essentially to *décadence*: the gap between man and man, between class and class, the multiplicity of types, the will to assert itself, to stand out in contrast, that which I call *pathos of distance* belongs to every *vigorous* period. The power of stretch, the width of stretch between the extremes, becomes always smaller at present,—the extremes themselves finally merge into similarity. All our political theories *and* state constitutions, the "German Empire" by no means excepted, are consequences, resulting necessities, of *décadence*; the unconscious operation of *décadence* has gained the ascendency so far as to affect the ideals of some of the sciences. My objection against the whole of the sociology of England and France is that it only knows *decaying types* of society by experience, and quite innocently takes its own instincts of decay as the standard for sociological valuations. *Deteriorating* life, the decline of all organising power (*i.e.* separating, gap-making, subordinating and superordinating power) is formulated as the *ideal*, in the sociology of the present day. Our socialists are *décadents*; Mr. Herbert Spencer, however, is also a *décadent*,—he sees something desirable in the triumph of altruism.

38

My concept of freedom.—The worth of a thing lies sometimes not in what one attains with it, but in what one pays for it,—what it *costs* us. I give an example. Liberal institutions immediately cease to be liberal, as soon as they are attained; afterwards, there are no more mischievous or more radical enemies of freedom than liberal institutions. One knows well enough *what* they accomplish: they undermine the will to power, they are the levelling of mountain and valley exalted into morality, they make people small, cowardly, and voluptuous,—with them the herding animal always triumphs. Liberalism: that is *increased herding-animality* . . . The same institutions produce quite other results as long as they are fought for; they then, in fact, further freedom in a powerful manner. On looking more accurately, we see that it is warfare which produces these results, warfare *for* liberal institutions, which, as war, allows *illiberal* instincts to continue. And warfare educates for freedom. For what is freedom? To have the will to be responsible for one's self. To keep the distance which separates us. To become more indifferent to hardship, severity, privation, and even to life. To be ready to sacrifice men for one's cause, one's self not excepted. Freedom implies that manly instincts, instincts which delight in war and triumph, dominate over other instincts; for example over the instincts of "happiness." The man *who has become free*, how much more the spirit which has become free, treads under foot the contemptible species of well-being dreamt of by shopkeepers, Christians, cows, women, Englishmen, and other democrats. The free man is a *warrior.*—How is freedom measured, in individuals, as well as in nations? By the resistance which has to be overcome, by the effort which it costs to retain superiority. We should have to seek the highest type of free men where the highest resistance is constantly overcome: five paces from tyranny, close on the threshold of the danger of thraldom. This is psychologically true, when we mean by "tyrants" pitiless and frightful instincts, which peremptorily call forth the maximum of authority and discipline—the finest type is furnished by Julius Cæsar; it is also politically true—let us but traverse the course of history. The people who were worth something, who *became* worth something, never acquired their greatness under liberal institutions: *great danger* made something out of them which deserves reverence,— danger which first teaches us to know our resources, our virtues, our shield and sword, our *genius,*—which *compels* us to be strong . . . *First* principle: men must require strength; otherwise, they never attain it.— Those great forcing-houses for the strong, the strongest species of man that has hitherto existed, the aristocratic commonwealths of the pattern of Rome and Venice, understood freedom precisely in the sense in which I understand the word: as something which one has and has *not,* as something which one *desires,* which one *wins by conquest* . . .

39

Criticism of modernism.—Our institutions are no longer worth anything: that is a matter on which we are unanimous. But the fault is not in the institutions, but in *us.* After we have lost all instincts out of which institutions grow, the institutions themselves are being lost, because *we* are no longer suitable for them. Democratism has always been the *dé-cadence* type of organising power: I have already (Human, All-too-human, Vol. I. Aphorism 472) characterised modern democracy (together with its incomplete forms, such as the "German Empire") as a *declining type of the state.* In order that there may be institutions, there must be a species of will, instinct, or imperative, antiliberal even to malignity: a will for tradition, for authority, for responsibility throughout centuries, a will for the *solidarity* of chains of generations forward and backward *in infinitum.* When this will exists, something establishes itself like the *Imperium Romanum;* or like Russia, the *only* power at present which has durability in its constitution, which can wait, and can yet promise something,—Russia, the antithetical conception to the pitiable European petty-state-misery and nervousness, which has got into a critical condition with the establishment of the German Empire . . . The entire western world no longer possesses those instincts out of which institutions grow, out of which *futurity* grows; perhaps nothing is so much against the grain of its "modern spirit." We live for the present, we live very fast,—we live very irresponsibly: this is precisely what we call "freedom." That which *makes* institutions in reality, is despised, hated, and repudiated: wherever the word "authority" even becomes audible, people believe themselves in danger of a new slavery. *Décadence* goes so far in the appreciative instinct of our politicians and political parties, that *they prefer instinctively* what disintegrates, what hastens the end . . . Witness *modern marriage*. All rationality has evidently been lost in modern marriage; that does not however furnish an objection against marriage, but against modernism. Rationality of marriage—it lay in the sole legal responsibility of the husband: marriage thus possessed gravity, while at present it halts on both legs. Rationality of marriage—it lay in its indissolubleness on principle: it thus acquired an emphasis which, opposed to the accident of sentiment, passion, and momentary impulse, knew how *to make itself heard*. Rationality of marriage—it lay likewise in the responsibility of families for the selection of the spouses. By the increasing indulgence in favour of marriages for *love*, the basis of marriage, that which first of all *makes* it an institution, has been almost eliminated. An institution is never, and never will be founded on an idiosyncrasy: marriage, as we have said, *cannot* be founded on "love,"—it is founded on sexual impulse, on the impulse to possess property (woman and child as property), on the *impulse to rule*, which constantly organises for itself the smallest type of sovereignty (family), which *needs* children and heirs to maintain physiologically an acquired measure of power, influence and riches, to prepare for long tasks, and for instinct-solidarity from one century to another. Marriage, as an institution, already involves the affirmation of the greatest and most permanent form of organisation: if society cannot as a whole *pledge* itself to the remotest generations, marriage has no meaning at all.—Modern marriage has *lost* its meaning,—consequently, it is being done away with.

40

The labour question.—The fact that there is a labour question is owing to stupidity, or, at bottom, instinct-degeneration, which is the cause of *all* existing stupidity. Regarding certain things *one does not question*: the first imperative of instinct.—I do not at all understand what people want to do with the European working man, now that they have made a question of him. He finds himself far too advantageously situated not to go on questioning *further*, ever less modestly. He has at last the majority on his side. There is no hope now that a modest and self-contented species of human being, a type like the Chinese, will here constitute itself into a class: this would have been the rational course, this would have been almost a necessity. But what have people done?— Everything possible to annihilate even the germ of the pre-requisite for such a course;—through the most unjustifiable thoughtlessness people have fundamentally destroyed the instincts in virtue of which the working man becomes possible as a class, possible *for himself.* The working man has been made capable of military service, he has been given the right of combination and the right of the franchise: no wonder he already feels his existence as a state of exigency (morally expressed, as *injustice*). But what do people *want?* let it be asked once more. If they want to realise an end, they must also be willing to use the means: if they want to have slaves, it is foolish to educate them to be masters.—

41

"*Freedom* which I do *not* mean[1] . . ."—In such times as the present, it is an additional peril to be left to one's instincts. These instincts mutually contradict, disturb, and destroy themselves; I have already defined *modernism* as physiological self-contradiction. A rational education would claim that one, at least, of those instinct-systems should be *paralysed* under an iron pressure, to enable another system to attain power, to become strong and predominant . . . At present one would have to make the individual possible in the first place, by *pruning* him. To make him possible, that is to say, to make him an *entirety* . . . The very reverse happens: independence, free development, and *laisser aller*, are claimed the most vehemently precisely by those for whom no restraint *would be too severe*—this is true *in politicis*, it is true in art. But that is a symptom of *décadence*: our modern notion of "freedom" is an additional proof of degeneration of instinct.—

42

Where belief is necessary.—Nothing is rarer among moralists and saints than rectitude; perhaps they say the contrary, perhaps they even *believe* it. For when a belief is more useful, more efficacious, and more convincing than *conscious* hypocrisy, owing to instinct, hypocrisy forthwith becomes *innocence*: first proposition for understanding great saints. Among philosophers also, another species of saints, the whole business involves the necessity of only admitting certain truths, namely those, on the basis of which their business has *public* sanction,—in Kantian language, the truths of *practical* reason. They know what they *must*

---

[1]An allusion to Max von Schenkendorf's poem: *Freiheit, die ich meine.*

prove, they are practical therein,—they recognise one another by being in mutual agreement with regard to "truths."—"Thou shalt not lie"— *i.e.* Mr. philosopher, *be on your guard*, lest you speak the truth . . .

43

Whispered into the ear of the conservatives. —What people did not know before, what they now know, or might know,—a *retrogression*, a return in any sense, or to any extent, is quite impossible. We physiologists, at least, know that. But all priests and moralists have believed it possible,—they *wanted* to bring mankind back, to *screw* mankind down to an *earlier* standard of virtue. Morality has always been a Procrustes-bed. Politicians even have imitated the preachers of virtue in this respect; at present also, there are parties who dream of the *crabs-march* of everything, as the final goal. No one, however, is at liberty to be a crab. There is no help for it: we are obliged to go forward, that is to say, *step by step onwards in décadence* (this is *my* definition of modern "progress" . . .) We can *check* this development, and by checking it, we can dam up and collect degeneration itself, making it more vehement and *sudden*; we cannot do more.—

44

My notion of genius. —Great men, like great periods, are explosive materials in which an immense force is accumulated; it is always prerequisite for such men, historically and physiologically, that for a long period there has been a collecting, a heaping up, an economising, and a hoarding, with respect to them,—that for a long time no explosion has taken place. When the tension in the substance has become too great, the most accidental stimulus suffices to call into the world the "genius," the "deed," and grand destiny. Of what consequence then is the environment, the epoch, the "spirit of the age," or "public opinion"!—Let us take the case of Napoléon. The France of the Revolution (and still more pre-revolutionary France) would have produced a type antithetical to Napoléon: it *did* produce it. And because Napoléon was of *a different type*, the heir of a stronger, more enduring, and older civilisation than that which vanished into vapour and fragments in France, he became master, he alone *was* the master here. The great men are necessary, the time when they appear is contingent; that they almost always become masters of their age, just depends on the fact that they are stronger, older, and possess longer accumulated forces. Between a genius and his age there exists a relation like that between the strong and the weak, between the old and the young: the age is, relatively, always much younger, more slender, more immature, more unassured, and more childish.—That people at present think *very differently* concerning this matter in France (and in Germany also, but that is of no consequence), that the theory of the *milieu*, a true neuropathic theory, has there become sacrosanct and almost scientific, finding belief even among physiologists—that "has a bad odour," it gives one melancholy thoughts.—In England also, the thing is understood in the very same manner; but nobody will fret about that. There are only two ways in which an Englishman can account for a genius or "great man:" either *democratically* in the manner of Buckle, or *religiously* in the manner of Carlyle.—The *peril* involved in great men and great ages is excessive; exhaustion of every kind, and sterility follow in their footsteps. The great man is a close; the great period, the Renaissance, for example, is a close. The genius—in work, in deed—is necessarily a squanderer; his greatness is *that he expends himself*. The instinct of self-preservation is, as it were, out of gear in the genius; the over-powerful pressure of the outflow of his energies forbids all such care and foresight. People call this "sacrifice," they praise the heroism of genius, his indifference to his own welfare, his devotion to an idea, to a great cause, or to his country: it is all misunderstanding, however . . . He outflows, he overflows, he uses himself up, he does not spare himself—fatefully, portentously, involuntarily, as a river involuntarily overflows its banks. But because people owe much to such explosives they have, on the other hand, bestowed much upon them; for example, a sort of *higher morality* . . . For that is the mode of human gratitude: it *misunderstands* its benefactors.—

45

The criminal and those related to him.—The criminal type—that is the type of the strong man under unfavourable conditions, a strong man who has been made sick. He lacks the wilderness, a certain freer and more dangerous environment, and mode of being, in which all that is offensive and defensive in his instincts *exists by right*. His *virtues* are put in ban by society; the most lively impulses instinctive to him become forthwith interwoven with depressing emotions,—with suspicion, fear, and disgrace. But this is almost the *recipe* for producing physiological degeneration. He who, with prolonged suspense, foresight, and cunning, has to do secretly what he can best do, what he would most readily do, becomes anæmic; and because he gains nothing but danger, persecution, and calamity through his instincts, his sentiment towards them quite alters: he regards them as fatalistic. It is society, our domesticated, mediocre, emasculated society, in which a man with his natural forces unimpaired, coming from the mountains or from sea-faring adventures, necessarily degenerates into a criminal. Or almost necessarily; for there are cases in which such a man proves himself stronger than society:—the Corsican Napoléon is the most celebrated case. For the problem before us, the testimony of Dostoiewsky is of importance—Dostoiewsky, the only psychologist, let it be said, from whom I had anything to learn; he belongs to the happiest chance incidents of my life, still more even than the discovering of Stendhal. This *profound* man, who was ten times right to depreciate the superficial Germans, has perceived that the Siberian convicts, in whose midst he lived for a long time (capital criminals for whom there was no return to society), were quite other than he himself expected,—persons carved almost out of the best, the hardest, and the most valuable material to be found in the Russian dominions. Let us generalise the case of the criminal: let us realise the disposition of persons, who, from any cause whatsoever, lack public approbation, who know that they are not regarded as salutary and serviceable to society,—that Chandala feeling of being counted inferior, outcast, unworthy, and defiling. All such natures have the colour of the subterranean, in their thoughts and actions; everything in them becomes paler than in those on whose existence daylight rests. But almost all modes of existence which we at present signalise, have formerly lived in this semi-sepulchral atmosphere,—the scientific man of character, the artist, the genius, the free spirit, the actor, the merchant, the great discoverer . . . As long as the *priest* passed for the highest type, *every* meritorious variety of human being was depreciated . . . The time comes—I promise it—when the priest will be regarded as the *lowest* type, as *our* Chandala, as the most mendacious, the most disreputable variety of human being . . . I direct attention to the fact that even at present (under the mildest sway of custom that has ever existed on earth, at least in Europe), every mode of separateness, every protracted, all-too-protracted *condition of subterposition*, every unusual, non-transparent mode of existence, approximates men to the type of which the criminal is the climax. All intellectual innovators have, for a time, the pale and portentous sign of the Chandala on their foreheads; *not* because they should be felt as such, but because they themselves are sensible of the frightful gulf which separates them from everything traditional and honourable. Almost every genius knows the "Catilinarian existence," as one of his developments, a hateful, revengeful, insurrectionary feeling against everything which already *is*, which does not any longer *become* . . . Catilina—the pre-existent form of *every* Cæsar. —

46

Here the prospect is open. —It may be loftiness of soul when a philosopher is silent; it may be love when he contradicts himself; in a knowing one a courtesy which speaks falsely is possible. It has been said not without acuteness: *il est indigne des grands cœurs de répandre le trouble, qu'ils ressentent*; only one has to add that it may likewise be greatness of soul to have no fear of *the meanest things.* A woman who loves, sacrifices her honour; a knowing one who "loves," perhaps sacrifices his humanity; a God who loved, became a Jew . . .

47

Beauty no accident.—Even the beauty of a race or family, the pleasantness and kindness of their whole demeanour, is acquired by effort; like genius, it is the final result of the accumulated labour of generations. There must have been great sacrifices made to good taste; for the sake of it, much must have been done, and much refrained from—the seventeenth century in France is worthy of admiration in both ways; good taste must then have been a principle of selection, for society, place, dress, and sexual gratification: beauty must have been preferred to advantage, habit, opinion, indolence. Supreme rule: we must not "let ourselves go," even when only in our own presence.—Good things are costly beyond measure, and the rule always holds, that he who possesses them is other than he who *acquires* them. All excellence is inheritance; what has not been inherited is imperfect, it is a beginning . . . At Athens in the time of Cicero, who expresses his surprise with regard to it, men and youths were far superior to women in beauty: but what labour and effort in the service of beauty had the Athenian males required of themselves for centuries!—We must not make a mistake here with regard to method: the mere rearing of feelings and thoughts is almost valueless (it is here that German culture, which is entirely illusory, makes its great mistake); we have first to persuade the *body.* The strict maintenance of significant and select demeanour, an obligation to live only with those who do not "let themselves go," suffices perfectly for becoming significant and select; in two or three generations everything has become *inwardised.* It is decisive for the fortune of a people and of humanity, that civilisation begins at the *right place*—*not* at "soul" (as was the baneful superstition of priests and semi-priests); the right place is body, demeanour, regimen, physiology; the *rest* follows therefrom. It is on that account that the Greeks are the *leading event* in the history of *civilisation*: they knew, they *did* what was necessary; Christianity, which despised the body, has hitherto been the greatest misfortune for the human race.—

48

Progress as I understand it.—I also speak of "return to nature," although it is not properly a going back, but a going up—up into high, free, and even frightful nature and naturalness, such as plays, *may* play with great tasks . . . To express it in a *simile*, Napoléon was an instance of a "return to nature," as I understand it (for example, *in rebus tacticis*, and still more in strategy, as military men are aware).—But Rousseau—where did he really want to return to? Rousseau, that first modern man, idealist and *canaille* in one person; needing moral "dignity" to endure his own aspect; sick with wanton conceit and wanton self-contempt! And even this abortion, which deposited itself on the threshold of the modern age, wanted "return to nature"—where, let us ask again, did Rousseau want to return to?—I hate Rousseau, hate him *in* the revolution itself: it is the grand historical expression of this dualism of idealist and *canaille*. The bloody *farce* with which that revolution played itself out, its "immorality," is of little account to me; what I hate is its Rousseau-*morality*—the so-called "truths" of the revolution with which it operates to the present day, and wins over to itself all the shallow and mediocre. The doctrine of equality! . . . But there exists no deadlier poison; for it *seems* to be preached by justice itself, while it *does away* with justice . . . "Equality to the equal, inequality to the unequal"—that would be the true teaching of justice; and the corollary likewise, "Never make the unequal equal."—That such dreadful and bloody events happened around the doctrine of equality, has given a sort of glory and luridness to this "modern idea" *par excellence*: so that the revolution as a *spectacle* has seduced even the noblest minds. That is, after all, no reason for esteeming it any higher.—I see only one who regarded it as it must be regarded, with *disgust*—Goethe . . .

49

Goethe.—No mere German event, but a European event; a grand attempt to surmount the eighteenth century, by a return to nature, by an *ascension* to the naturalness of the Renaissance, a kind of self-surmounting on the part of that century.—He possessed its strongest instincts: its sentimentality, its nature worship, its tendencies antihistoric, idealistic, unreal, and revolutionary (the last is only a form of the unreal). He called to his aid history, science, antiquity, and likewise Spinoza, but above all practical activity; he encircled himself with nothing but defined horizons; he did not sever himself from life, but placed himself in it; he was not desponding, and took as much as possible on himself, over himself, and into himself. What he aspired to was *totality*; he struggled against the severance of reason, sensuousness, emotion and will (preached in the most forbidding scholasticism by *Kant*, the antipode of Goethe), he disciplined himself to entirety, he *created* himself . . . Goethe was a convinced realist in the midst of an age disposed to the unreal; he was affirmative of everything analogous to himself in this respect,—he had no more important experience than that *ens realissimum*, named Napoléon. Goethe conceived of a personality robust and high-cultured, skilful in all physical accomplishments, keeping himself in check, and maintaining his self-reverence, who dares to allow himself the whole realm and riches of naturalness, and is strong enough for that freedom; the man of toleration, not out of weakness, but out of strength, because he knows how to use advantageously what would cause the ruin of average constitutions; the man to whom there is nothing prohibited—unless it be *weakness*,—whether it is designated vice or virtue. . . . A mind thus *emancipated* stands with a cheerful and confident fatalism in the midst of the universe, in the *belief* that only the single thing is rejectable, that, on the whole, everything is saved and maintained: *he no longer denies* . . . But such a belief is the highest of all possible beliefs: I have christened it with the name of *Dionysos.—*

50

We might say that, in a certain sense, the nineteenth century has likewise aspired after all that Goethe himself aspired after: universality in understanding and approving, a quiet reserve towards everything, an audacious realism, and reverence for all matters of fact. How is it that the sum total is no Goethe, but a chaos, a nihilistic groaning, a grievous uncertainty as to whence and whither, an instinctive weariness which *in praxi* impels men continually *to hark back to the eighteenth century?* (For example, as emotional Romanticism, as altruism, as hyper-sentimentality, as feminism in taste, and as socialism in politics.) Is not the nineteenth century, especially at its close, merely a strengthened and *brutalised* eighteenth century, *i.e.* a *décadence* century? So that Goethe would have been merely an episode, a splendid, vain effort, not only for Germany, but for Europe as a whole? But we misunderstand great men when we look at them from the narrow perspective of public utility. That we do not know how to derive advantage from them—*that itself perhaps belongs to greatness* . . .

51

Goethe is the last German for whom I have reverence; he would have felt three things which I feel,—we also understand one another with regard to the "cross" . . . People often ask me why in the world I write in

German: I was nowhere less read than in my own country. But who knows, after all, if I even *want* to be read at present? — To create things on which time vainly tries its teeth; as regards form, *as regards substance,* to make an effort after a little immortality. I was never yet modest enough to require less of myself. Aphorism and the sentence, in which I, as the foremost among the Germans, am master, are the forms of "eternity;" my ambition is to say in ten sentences what everyone else says in a book, — what everyone else does *not* say in a book . . .

I have given to mankind the profoundest book it possesses, my *Zarathushtra:* I shall shortly give it the most independent one.

MY INDEBTEDNESS TO THE ANCIENTS

1

A word in conclusion with regard to that world to which I have sought access, to which I have perhaps found a new entrance,—the ancient world. My taste, which may be the contrary of a tolerant taste, is here, as in other cases, far from making an unconditional affirmation: on the whole, it does not readily say yea; it rather prefers nay; it likes best of all to say nothing whatever . . . This applies to entire civilisations, it applies to books,—it applies also to places and landscapes. After all it is only a very small number of ancient books that count in my life; the most celebrated ones are not among them. My sense for style, for the epigram as style, awakened almost instantaneously on coming in contact with Sallust. I have not forgotten the astonishment of my venerated teacher Corssen, when he had to give the highest number of marks to his worst Latin scholar,—I had done all at once. Compressed, rigid, with as much substance as possible in the background, a cool malice against "fine words" and "fine sentiment" also,—I therewith found my vein. In my writings up to my *Zarathushtra*, a very strenuous ambition to attain the *Roman* style, the "*ære perennius*" in style will be recognised.—It was the same with me on my first contact with Horace. Up to the present, I have not received from any poet the same artistic rapture as was given to me from the first by an Horatian ode. In certain languages that which is attained there cannot even *be willed*. That lingual mosaic where every word, as sound, as position, and as notion, diffuses its force right, left, and over the whole, that *minimum* in the compass and number of signs, that *maximum* thus realised in their energy,—all that is Roman, and, if you will believe me, it is *noble par excellence*. All other poetry becomes somewhat too popular in comparison with it,—mere sentimental loquacity.

2

I am not at all under obligation to the Greeks for any similarly strong

70

impressions, and, to speak out candidly, they *cannot* be to us what the Romans are. We do not *learn* from the Greeks: their mode is too foreign, it is also too unstable to operate imperatively or "classically." Who would ever have learned to write from a Greek! Who would ever have learned it *without* the Romans! . . . Plato need not be brought forward as an objection to me. With respect to Plato, I am a thorough sceptic, and I have always been unable to assent to the admiration of Plato the *artist*, which is traditional among scholars. After all, I have here the most refined judges of taste among the ancients themselves on my side. Plato, as it seems to me, jumbles together all the forms of style; he is thus a *first décadent* in style: he has something on his conscience like what the Cynics have, who discovered the *satura Menippea*. To be operated upon by the Platonic dialogue — that shockingly self-complacent and childish kind of dialectics, — a person must never have read good French literature, — Fontenelle, for example. Plato is tiresome. — In the end my distrust of Plato goes deeper than the surface: I find him strayed so far from all fundamental instincts of the Hellenes, so mismoralised, so pre-existently Christian (he has already the concept "good" as the highest concept), that I should prefer to employ the hard expression, "superior cheatery," with reference to the whole phenomenon of Plato (or, if people like it better, idealism), rather than any other term. People have paid dearly for this Athenian's going to school with the Egyptians (or with the Jews in Egypt? . . .). In the great fatality of Christianity, Plato is the ambiguity and fascination called the "ideal," which made it possible for the nobler minds of antiquity to misunderstand themselves, and enter on the *bridge* which led to the "cross" . . . And how much of Plato is still in the conception of "Church," in the organisation, system, and practice of the Church! — My recreation, my predilection, my *cure* from all Platonism, has always been *Thucydides*. Thucydides, and perhaps Macchiavelli's *Principe* are nearest akin to me in the unconditioned will to impose nothing on themselves, and in their determination to see the rational in *reality*, — *not* in "reason," and still less in "morality" . . . There is no better corrective than Thucydides of the pitiable tendency to beautify the Greeks in the direction of the ideal, a tendency which the youth "trained in humanities" carries away with him into life as the reward of his public-school drilling. One has to turn his writings over line by line, and read his mental reserve as distinctly as his words: there are few thinkers so rich in mental reserve. *Sophist civilisation*, I mean to say *realist civilisation*, attains its most perfect expression in Thucydides: that inestimable movement in the midst of the moral and ideal cheatery of the Socratic Schools, which, just then, was breaking out everywhere. Greek philosophy as the *décadence* of Greek instinct; Thucydides as the great sum, the last revelation of that strong, stern, hard matter-of-factness, which was instinctive in the older Hellenes. *Courage* in presence of reality distinguishes in the end such natures as Thucydides from Plato: Plato is a coward in presence of reality,—*consequently* he takes refuge in the ideal; Thucydides is master of *himself*, consequently he maintains power also over things . . .

3

To scent out "beautiful souls," "golden mediocrities," and other perfections in the Greeks, perhaps to admire in them the repose in grandeur, the ideal disposition, lofty simplicity—from this "lofty simplicity" (a *niaiserie allemande* in the end), I was preserved by the psychologist implanted in my nature. I saw their strongest instinct, the will to power, I saw them quake in presence of the intractable force of this impulse,— I saw all their institutions evolve out of protective measures to secure themselves mutually from their innate *explosive material*. The enormous internal tension then discharged itself externally, in dreadful and reckless hostility: the city communities lacerated themselves in conflict with one another, in order that the citizens of each might find peace within themselves. People required to be strong; danger was close at hand,—it lurked everywhere. The magnificently supple physique, the daring realism and immoralism which belonged to the Hellene, were an *exigency*, not a "temperament." These qualities only came in course of time, they were not there from the beginning. And the Greeks desired naught else but to feel themselves *dominant*, to *show* themselves dominant with their festivals and arts: these things were expedients for self-glorification, under certain circumstances for inspiring terror . . . To judge the Greeks by their philosophers in the German manner, to avail one's self perchance of the affected virtuousness of the Socratic Schools for disclosures as to *what* is fundamentally Hellenic! . . . For the philosophers are the *décadents* of Grecianism, the countermovement against ancient, noble taste (against the agonal instinct, against the *polis*, against the worth of the race, against the authority of tradition). Socratic virtues were preached *because* they had been lost by the Greeks: excitable, timid, fickle, all of them comedians, they had a few reasons too many for allowing morality to be preached to them. Not that it did help anything, but great words and attitudes suit *décadents* so well . . .

4

I was the first for the purpose of understanding the older, still copious, and even overflowing Hellenic instinct, to take seriously that wonderful phenomenon which bears the name of Dionysos: it is only explainable by a *surplus* of energy. Whoever had devoted his attention to the Greeks,—like that profoundest student of their civilisation at present living, Jacob Burckhardt of Bâle,—was at once aware that something has been achieved thereby: Burckhardt inserted a special chapter into his "Kultur der Griechen" on the phenomenon referred to. If one wants the contrast one may look at the almost exhilarating poverty of instinct in German philologists, when they come into proximity with the Dionysian. The celebrated Lobeck especially, who, with the venerable assurance of a worm dried up between books, crept into this world of mysterious conditions, and, by being frivolous and childish *ad nauseam*, persuaded himself that he was scientific,—Lobeck, with great display of learning, has given to understand that it is really no matter about all these curiosities. In fact, the priests might have communicated some not unimportant information to those who took part in such orgies; for example, that wine excites lust, that under certain circumstances man lives on fruit, that plants blossom in spring and wither in autumn. As regards that strange wealth of rites, symbols, and myths of orgiastic origin with which the ancient world is literally overgrown, Lobeck finds in it an occasion to become a trifle more ingenious. "The Greeks," he says (*Aglaophamus* I. 672) "when they had nothing else to do, laughed, jumped, and raged about, or, because people have also sometimes a desire for that, they sat down, wept, and lamented. *Others* came there later on, and sought, sure enough, some reason for the strange behaviour; and thus the numberless festival legends and myths arose for the explanation of those practices. On the other hand, people believed that that *ludicrous performance* which took place by custom on the festive days, belonged necessarily to festal celebration, and they retained it as an indispensable part of Divine worship."—That is contemptible gossip, one will not for a moment take Lobeck seriously. We are affected quite otherwise when we examine the concept of "Grecian" which Winckelmann and Goethe had formed for themselves, and when we find it incompatible with that element—orgiasm—out of which Dionysian art evolves. In fact, I do not doubt that Goethe would have thoroughly excluded anything of that kind from the potentialities of the Greek soul. *Consequently, Goethe did not understand the Greeks.* For only in Dionysian mysteries, in the psychology of the Dionysian condition, does the *fundamental fact* of Hellenic instinct—its "will to life"—express itself. *What* did the Hellene pledge himself for with these mysteries? *Eternal* life, eternal recurrence of life; the future promised and consecrated in the past; the triumphing affirmation of life beyond death and change; *true* life, as the universal continuation of life by generation, by the mysteries of sexuality. On that account, the *sexual* symbol was to the Greeks the symbol venerable in itself, the intrinsic profundity within all ancient piety. Every detail in the act of generation, in pregnancy, and in birth, awakened the most exalted and solemn sentiments. In the doctrine of mysteries *pain* is pronounced holy: the "pains of travail" sanctify pain in general,—all becoming and growing, all pledging for the future, *involves* suffering . . . In order that the eternal delight of creating may exist, that the will to life may assert itself eternally, there *must* also exist eternally the "pains of travail." All this is implied by the word Dionysos: I know of no higher symbolism than this *Greek* symbolism of *Dionysia*. In them the deepest instinct of life, the instinct for the future of life, for the eternity of life, is felt religiously—the way itself to life, procreation, is recognised as the *sacred* way . . . It is only Christianity, with its resentment *against* life at the bottom, which has caused sexuality to be regarded as something impure: it cast *dirt* on the commencement, on the pre-requisite of our life . . .

5

The psychology of orgiasm, as an exuberant feeling of life and energy, in which pain even operates as a stimulus, gave me the key to the concept of *tragic* feeling which has been misunderstood, as well by Aristotle, as especially by our pessimists. Tragedy is so far from proving anything with regard to a pessimism of the Hellenes, in the sense of Schopenhauer, that it is rather to be looked upon as the decisive repudiation of pessimism, and as a *verdict against* it. The affirmation of life, even in its most unfamiliar and most severe problems, the will to life, enjoying its own inexhaustibility in the *sacrifice* of its highest types,— *that* is what I called Dionysian, *that* is what I divined as the bridge to a psychology of the *tragic* poet. Not in order to get rid of terror and pity, not to purify from a dangerous passion by its vehement discharge (it was thus that Aristotle understood it); but, beyond terror and pity, *to realise in fact* the eternal delight of becoming,—that delight which even involves in itself the *joy of annihilating* . . . And hereby I again touch at the place from which I once set out,—the "Birth of Tragedy" was my first Transvaluation of all Values: hereby I place myself again on the soil out of which my willing, my *ability* has evolved—I, the last disciple of Dionysos the philosopher,—I, the teacher of eternal recurrence . . .

THE HAMMER SPEAKETH

Thus Spake Zarathushtra. III.
Of the Spirit of Gravity, 29.

"Why so hard!" said once the charcoal unto the diamond, "are we not near relations?"

Why so soft? Oh my brethren, thus I ask you. Are ye not — my brethren?

Why so soft, so unresisting, and yielding? Why is there so much disavowal and abnegation in your hearts? Why is there so little fate in your looks?

And if you are unwilling to be fates, and inexorable, how could you — conquer with me someday?

And if your hardness would not glance, and cut, and chip to pieces, how could you — create with me someday?

For all creators are hard. And it must seem blessedness unto you to press your hand upon millenniums as upon wax, —

— Blessedness to write upon the will of millenniums as upon brass, — harder than brass, nobler than brass. The noblest only is perfectly hard.

This new table, oh my brethren, I put over you: Become hard! —

THE ANTICHRIST:
AN ESSAY TOWARDS
A CRITICISM OF CHRISTIANITY

PREFACE

This book belongs to the select few. Perhaps even none of them yet live. They may be those who understand my *Zarathushtra*: how *could* I confound myself with those for whom ears are growing at present?— It is only the day after to-morrow that belongs to me. Some are born posthumously.

The conditions under which a person understands me, and then *necessarily* understands,—I know them only too accurately. He must be honest in intellectual matters even to sternness, in order even to endure my seriousness, my passion. He must be accustomed to live on mountains—to see the wretched ephemeral gossip of politics and national egotism *under* him. He must have become indifferent, he must never ask whether truth is profitable or becomes a calamity to him . . . A predilection of robustness for questions for which at present no one has the courage; the courage for the *forbidden*; the predetermination for the labyrinth. An experience out of seven solitudes. New ears for new music. New eyes for the most distant. A new conscience for truths which have hitherto remained dumb. *And* the will for economy in the grand style: to keep together one's power, one's *enthusiasm* . . . Reverence for one's self; love to one's self; unconditioned freedom with respect to one's self . . .

Well then! Those alone are my readers, my right readers, my predetermined readers: of what account are the *rest?*—The rest are merely mankind.—One must be superior to mankind in force, in loftiness of soul,—in contempt . . .

FRIEDRICH NIETZSCHE.

1

—Let us look one another in the face. We are Hyperboreans—we know well enough how much out of the way we live. "Neither by land nor by water wilt thou find the way to the Hyperboreans:" Pindar already knew that of us. Beyond the north, beyond ice, beyond death—*our* life, *our* happiness . . . We have discovered happiness, we know the way, we have found the exit from entire millenniums of labyrinth. Who has found it besides?—Modern man perhaps?—"I do not know out or in; I am whatever does not know out or in"—sighs modern man . . . We were ill from *that* modernism,—from lazy peace, from cowardly compromise, from the whole virtuous uncleanness of modern yea and nay. That tolerance and *largeur* of heart which "forgives" all because it "understands" all, is Sirocco to us. Better to live in the ice than among modern virtues and other south-winds! . . . We were brave enough, we spared neither ourselves nor others; but we did not know for a long time *where* to direct our bravery. We became gloomy, were called fatalists. *Our* fate—that was the fulness, the tension, the damming up of our forces. We thirsted for lightning and for achievement, we were furthest removed from the happiness of weaklings, from "resignation" . . . A tempest was in our atmosphere; nature which we embody was darkened,—*for we had no path*. The formula of our happiness: a yea, a nay, a straight line, a *goal* . . .

2

What is good?—All that increases the feeling of power, will to power, power itself, in man.

What is bad?—All that proceeds from weakness.

What is happiness?—The feeling that power *increases*,—that a resistance is overcome.

Not contentedness, but more power; *not* peace at any price, but warfare; *not* virtue, but capacity (virtue in the Renaissance style, *virtù*, virtue free from any moralic acid).

The weak and ill-constituted shall perish: first principle of *our* charity. And people shall help them to do so.

What is more injurious than any crime?—Practical sympathy for all the ill-constituted and weak:—Christianity . . .

3

The problem which I here put is not what is to replace mankind in the chain of beings (man is an *end*), but what type of man we are to *cultivate*, we are to *will*, as the more valuable, the more worthy of life, the more certain of the future.

This more valuable type has often enough existed already: but as a happy accident, as an exception, never as *willed*. It has rather just been the most feared; it has hitherto been almost *the* terror;—and out of that terror, the reverse type has been willed, cultivated, *attained*; the domestic animal, the herding animal, the sickly animal man,—the Christian . . .

4

Mankind does not manifest a development to the better, the stronger, or the higher, in the manner in which it is at present believed. "Progress" is merely a modern idea, *i.e.* a false idea. The European of the present is, in worth, far below the European of the Renaissance; onward development is by *no* means, by any necessity, elevating, enhancing, strengthening.

In another sense, there is a continuous success of single cases in the most different parts of earth, and from the most different civilisations, in which, in fact, a *higher type* manifests itself: something which, in relation to collective mankind, is a sort of beyond-man. Such happy accidents of grand success have always been possible, and will, perhaps, always be possible. And even entire races, tribes, and nations can, under certain circumstances, represent such a *good hit*.

5

We must not embellish or deck out Christianity: it has waged a *deadly war* against this higher type of man, it has put in ban all fundamental instincts of this type, it has distilled evil, *the* evil one, out of these instincts:—strong man as the typical reprobate, as "out-cast man." Christianity has taken the part of all the weak, the low, the ill-constituted, it has made an ideal out of the *antagonism* to the preservative instincts of strong life; it has ruined the reason even of the intellectually strongest natures, in that it taught men to regard the highest values of intellectuality as sinful, as misleading, as *temptations*. The most lamentable example: the ruin of Pascal, who believed in the ruin of his intellect by original sin, while it had only been ruined by his Christianity! —

6

It is a painful and thrilling spectacle that has presented itself to me: I have drawn back the curtain from the *depravity* of man. This word in my mouth is, at all events, guarded against one suspicion: that it involves a moral accusation of man. It is — I should like to underline it once more — meant in the sense of freedom from any moralic acid and this to the extent that that depravity is felt by me most strongly just there, where one hitherto most consciously aspired to "virtue" and "Divinity." I understand depravity, one makes it out already, in the sense of *décadence*: my assertion is that all values in which mankind now comprise their highest desirability are *décadence-values*.

I call an animal, a species, an individual depraved, when it loses its instincts, when it selects, when it *prefers* what is injurious to it. A history of "higher sentiments," of "ideals of mankind" — and it is possible that I shall have to tell it again, — would be almost the explanation also *why* man is so depraved. Life itself I regard as instinct for growth, for continuance, for accumulation of forces, for *power*: where the will to power is wanting there is decline. My assertion is that this will *is lacking* in all the highest values of mankind, — that values of decline, *nihilistic* values, bear rule under the holiest names.

7

Christianity is called the religion of *sympathy*. — Sympathy stands in antithesis to the tonic passions which elevate the energy of the feeling of life: it operates depressively. One loses force by sympathising. The loss of force, which suffering has already brought upon life, is still further increased and multiplied by sympathy. Suffering itself becomes contagious through sympathy; under certain circumstances a total loss of life and vital energy may be brought about by sympathy, such as stands in an absurd proportion to the extent of the cause (the case of the death of the Nazarene). That is the first point of view; there is however one still more important. Supposing one measures sympathy according to the value of the reaction which, as a rule, it brings about, its mortally dangerous character appears in a much clearer light still. Sympathy thwarts, on the whole, in general, the law of development, which is the law of *selection*. It preserves what is ripe for extinction, it resists in favour of life's disinherited and condemned ones, it gives to life itself a gloomy and questionable aspect by the abundance of the ill-constituted of all kinds whom it *maintains* in life. One has dared to call sympathy a virtue (in every *superior* morality it is regarded as a weakness); one has gone further, one has made it *the* virtue, the basis and source of all virtues, — only, to be sure (which one must always keep in sight) from the point of view of a philosophy which was nihilistic, which inscribed the *negation of life* on its escutcheon! Schopenhauer was right in maintaining that life was negatived by sympathy, was made *worthier of negation*, — sympathy is the *practice* of nihilism. Once more repeated: this depressive and contagious instinct thwarts those instincts which strive for the maintenance and elevation of the value of life: it is, both as the *multiplier* of misery and as the *conservator* of all misery, a principal tool for the advancement of *décadence*, — sympathy persuades to *nothingness!* . . . One does not say *"nothingness:"* one says instead, "the other world;" or "God;" or "true life;" or Nirvana; salvation, blessedness . . . This innocent rhetoric, out of the domain of religio-moral idiosyncrasy, appears forthwith *much less innocent*, when one understands *what* tendency here wraps around itself the mantle of sublime expressions; the tendency *hostile to life*. Schopenhauer was hostile to life: *therefore* sympathy became to him a virtue . . . Aristotle, as is known, saw in sympathy a sickly and dangerous condition, which one did well now and then to get at by a purgative: he understood tragedy as a purgative. From the instinct of life, one should in fact seek an expedient to put a puncture in such a morbid and dangerous accumulation of sympathy as the case of Schopenhauer manifests (and alas also, our entire literary and artistic *décadence* from St. Petersburg to Paris, from Tolstoi to Wagner), that that bubble might burst . . . Nothing amidst our unsound modernism is unsounder than Christian sympathy. To be a physician *here*, to be pitiless *here*, to apply the knife *here* — that belongs to *us*, that is *our* mode of charity; thereby *we* are philosophers, we Hyperboreans! ——

8

It is necessary to say *whom* we regard as our antithesis: — theologians, and everything that has theological blood in its veins — our entire philosophy . . . One must have seen the fatality close at hand, or, better still, one must have experienced it in one's self, one must have been almost ruined by it, to regard it no longer as a jocular affair (the free-thinking of Messrs. our naturalists and physiologists is in my eyes a *joke* — they lack passionateness in these matters, the suffering from them). That poisoning extends far wider than one supposes; I discovered the theological instinct of haughtiness everywhere where people at present regard themselves as "idealists," — where, in virtue of a higher origin, they assume the right to cast looks superior and strange at actuality . . . The idealist, precisely like the priest, has all the great concepts in his hand (and not in his hand only), he plays them with a benevolent contempt against the "understanding," the "senses," "honours," "good living," and "science;" he sees such *under* him, as injurious and seductive forces, over which "spirit" soars in pure being-by-itself!—as if submissiveness, chastity, poverty, in a word *holiness* had not hitherto done unutterably more injury to life than any frightful things or vices . . . Pure spirit is pure lie . . . As long as the priest still passes for a *higher* species of human being,—this denier, calumniator, and poisoner of life by *profession*,—there is no answer to the question. What *is* truth? Truth *has been* already reversed when the conscious advocate of nothingness and denial passes for the representative of truth . . .

9

I make war against this theological instinct: I have found traces of it everywhere. Whoever has theological blood in his veins is from the very beginning ambiguous and disloyal with respect to everything. The pathos which develops therefrom calls itself belief: the closing of the eye once for all with respect to one's self, so as not to suffer from the sight—of incurable falsity. A person makes for himself a morality, a virtue, a sanctity out of this erroneous perspective towards all things, he unites the good conscience to the *false* mode of seeing,—he demands that no *other* mode of perspective be any longer of value, after he has made his own sacrosanct with the names of "God," "salvation," and "eternity." I have digged out the theologist-instinct everywhere; it is the most diffused, the most peculiarly *subterranean* form of falsity that exists on earth. What a theologian feels as true, *must* needs be false: one has therein almost a criterion of truth. It is his most fundamental self-preservative instinct which forbids reality to be held in honour, or even to find expression on any point. As far as theologist-influence extends, the *judgment of value* is turned right about, the concepts of "true" and "false" are necessarily reversed: what is most injurious to life is here called "true," what raises, elevates, affirms, justifies, and makes it triumph is called "false" . . . If it happens that, through the "conscience" of princes (or of the people), theologians stretch out their hand for *power*, let us not doubt *what* always takes place at bottom: the will to the end, *nihilistic* will seeks power . . .

10

Among Germans it is immediately understood when I say that philosophy is spoiled by theological blood. The Protestant clergyman is the grandfather of German philosophy, Protestantism itself is its *peccatum originale*. Definition of Protestantism: the half-sided paralysis of Christianity—*and* reason . . . One has only to utter the words "College of Tübingen" to comprehend what German philosophy is at bottom— *insidious* divinity . . . The Swabians are the best liars in Germany, they lie innocently . . . Whence the exaltation all over the German learned world (three-fourths of which is composed of the sons of clergymen and teachers) on the appearance of *Kant*,—whence the German conviction, which even still finds its echo, that with Kant a change for the *better* commenced? The theologist-instinct in German scholars made out *what* was now once more possible . . . a back-door path to the old ideal now stood open, the concept of a "true world," the concept of morality as *essence* of the world (these two most virulent errors that exist!) were again, thanks to a wily-shrewd scepticism, if not demonstrable, at least no longer *refutable* . . . Reason, the *prerogative* of reason does not reach so far . . . A "seemingness" had been made out of reality; a world, completely fabricated by a lie, the world of "what is," had been made reality . . . The success of Kant is merely a theologist success: Kant, like Luther and like Leibniz, was an additional drag on not-too-sound German uprightness:——

11

A word yet against Kant as a *moralist*. A virtue must be *our* contrivance, *our* most personal self-defence and necessity: in every other sense it is merely a danger. What does not condition our life *injures* it: a virtue merely out of a sentiment of respect for the concept of "virtue," as Kant would have it, is injurious. "Virtue," "duty," "the good in itself," the good with the character of impersonalness and universal validity— chimeras, in which the decline, the final debilitating of life, Königsbergian Chinaism, express themselves. The very reverse is commanded by the most fundamental laws of maintenance and growth: that everyone devise *his own* virtue, *his own* categorical imperative for himself. A people perishes when it confounds *its* duty with the general concept of duty. Nothing ruins more profoundly, or more intrinsically than every "impersonal" duty, every sacrifice before the Moloch of abstraction.— I wonder that Kant's categorical imperative has not been felt as *dangerous to life!* . . . The theologist-instinct alone took it under protection! An action to which the instinct of life impels has in its pleasure the proof that it is a *right* action: and that nihilist, with Christian-dogmatic intestines, understood pleasure as an *objection* . . . What destroys faster than to work, think, or feel without internal necessity, without a profoundly personal choice, without *pleasure?* as an automaton of "duty"? It is precisely the *recipe* for *décadence*, even for idiocy . . . Kant became an idiot.—And that was the contemporary of *Goethe!* And this calamity of a cobweb-spinner passed for the *German* philosopher,—passes for it still! . . . I take care not to say what I think of the Germans . . . Has not Kant seen in the French Revolution the transition from the inorganic form of the state into the *organic?* Did he not ask himself if there was an event which could not be explained otherwise than by a moral faculty in mankind, so that "the tendency of mankind to goodness" was *proved* by it once for all? Kant's answer: "That is revolution." The erring instinct in each and everything, antinaturalness as an instinct, German *décadence* as a philosophy—*that is Kant!*—

12

I put a few sceptics apart, the decent type in the history of philosophy: the remainder are ignorant of the first requirements of intellectual uprightness. All of them do just like little women, all those great enthusiasts and prodigies,—they regard "fine feelings" as arguments, the "expanded bosom" as the bellows of Divinity, conviction as a *criterion* of truth. In the end Kant attempted, with "German" innocence, to make scientific this form of corruption, this lack of intellectual conscience, under the concept of "practical reason:" he devised a reason expressly for the occasions in which one has not to trouble one's self about reason, namely, when morality, when the sublime requirement "thou shalt" becomes audible. If one considers that, almost among all nations, the philosopher is only the further development of the priestly type, this inheritance of the priest, the *spurious, self-imposed coinage*, no longer surprises one. When one has holy tasks, for example, to improve, to save, or to redeem men, when one carries Divinity in one's breast, when one is the mouth-piece of other-world imperatives,—with such a mission one is already outside of all merely reasonable valuations, one's self is already consecrated by such a task, it is already the type of a higher order! . . . What does the priest care for science! He stands too high for it!—And the priest has hitherto *ruled!*—He has *determined* the concepts of "true" and "untrue!" . . .

13

Let us not underestimate this: *we ourselves*, we free spirits, are already a "Transvaluation of all Values," an *incarnate* declaration of war against and triumph over all old concepts of "true" and "untrue." The most precious discernments into things are the latest discovered: the most precious discernments, however, are the *methods*. All methods, *all* presuppositions of our present-day science, have for millenniums been held in the most profound contempt: by reason of them a person was excluded from intercourse with "honest" men,—he passed for an "enemy of God," a despiser of truth, a "possessed" person. As a scientific man, a person was a Chandala . . . We have had the entire pathos of mankind against us,—their concept of that which truth *ought* to be, which the service of truth *ought* to be: every "thou shalt" has been hitherto directed *against* us. Our objects, our practices, our quiet, prudent, mistrustful mode—all appeared to mankind as absolutely unworthy and contemptible.—In the end one might, with some reasonableness, ask one's self if it was not really an æsthetic taste which kept mankind in such long blindness: they wanted a *picturesque* effect from truth, they wanted in like manner the knowing ones to operate strongly on their senses. Our *modesty* was longest against the taste of mankind . . . Oh how they made that out, these turkey-cocks of God——

14

We have counter-learned. We have become more modest in everything. We no longer derive man from "spirit," from "godhead," we have put him back among animals. We regard him as the strongest animal because he is the most cunning: his intellectuality is a consequence thereof. We guard ourselves, on the other hand, against a conceit which would fain be heard here once more: just as if man had been the great secret purpose of zoölogical evolution. He is by no means a crown of creation; every being along with him is at an equal stage of perfection . . . And when we make that assertion, we still assert too much: man is, taken relatively, the worst constituted animal, the most sickly, the most dangerously strayed from his instincts—to be sure with all that, also the *most interesting!*—As regards animals Descartes was the first, who, with a boldness worthy of reverence, ventured the idea of conceiving of the animal as *machina*: our entire physiology interests itself about the proof of this proposition. And, logically, we do not put man apart as Descartes did: whatever till now has been apprehended with regard to man reaches so far precisely as he has been apprehended mechanically. Formerly one gave man "free will" as his dowry out of a higher order: at present we have taken even will from him, in the sense that no faculty can any longer be understood under the term. The old word "will" serves only to designate a resultant, a kind of individual reaction which necessarily follows upon a number of partly antagonistic, partly congruous stimuli:—will no longer "works," it no longer "moves" . . . Formerly one saw in man's consciousness, in "spirit," the proof of his higher origin, of his Divinity; in order to *perfect* man, one advised him, after the manner of the tortoise to withdraw the senses into himself, to cease having intercourse with the earthly, to shuffle off the mor-

tal coil: then the main part of him remained behind, "pure spirit." We
have also given better thought to this matter: the fact of becoming conscious, "spirit," is regarded by us just as a symptom of the relative in-
completeness of the organism, as an attempting, groping, mistaking, as
a trouble by which unnecessarily much nerve-force is used up,—we
deny that anything whatsoever can be made perfect as long as it is still
made conscious. "Pure spirit" is a pure stupidity; when we deduct the
nervous system and the senses, the "mortal coil," *our calculation is
wrong*—that is all! . . .

15

In Christianity neither morality nor religion is in contact with any
point of actuality. Nothing but imaginary *causes* ("God," "soul," "ego,"
"spirit," "free will"—or even "unfree will"); nothing but imaginary *ef-
fects* ("sin," "salvation," "grace," "punishment," "forgiveness of sin"). An
intercourse between imaginary *beings* ("God," "spirits," "souls"); an
imaginary science of *nature* (anthropocentric; absolute lack of the concept of natural causes); an imaginary *psychology* (nothing but self-
misunderstandings, interpretations of pleasant or unpleasant general
feelings, for example, the conditions of the *nervus sympathicus*, with
the help of the sign-language of religio-moral idiosyncrasy,—"repen-
tance," "remorse of conscience," "temptation by the devil," "presence
of God"); an imaginary *teleology* ("the kingdom of God," "the last judgment," "everlasting life").—This purely *fictitious world* is, greatly to its
disadvantage, distinguished from the dream-world, in that while the latter *reflects* actuality, the *former* falsifies, depreciates, and negatives it.
When once the concept of "nature" was devised as a concept antithetical to "God," "natural" had to be the word for "reprehensible;"—that
whole fictitious world has its root in *hatred* against the natural (actuality!), it is the expression of a profound dissatisfaction with the actual . . .
But everything is explained thereby. Who alone has reasons for *lying*
himself *out of* actuality? He who *suffers* from it. But to suffer from
actuality is to be an *ill-constituted* actuality . . . The preponderance of
unpleasurable feelings over pleasurable feelings is the *cause* of that fictitious morality and religion: such a preponderance, however, furnishes
the *formula* for *décadence* . . .

16

A criticism of the *Christian concept of God* compels us to the same conclusion. A people which still believes in itself has withal its own God.
In him it reverences the conditions by which it is to the fore, its
virtues;—it projects its delight in itself, its feeling of power, into a being

who can be thanked for them. He who is rich wishes to bestow; a proud people needs a God in order to *sacrifice* . . . Religion, within the limits of such presuppositions, is a form of gratitude. One is thankful for one's self: for that purpose one needs a God.—Such a God must be able to be both serviceable and injurious, he must be able to be friend and foe,—he is admired alike in the good and in the bad. The *anti-natural* castration of a God to a God merely of the good would here be beyond the bounds of all desirability. The bad God is as necessary as the good God; for one does not owe one's existence to tolerance and humanitarianism . . . What would a God be worth who did not know anger, revenge, jealousy, scorn, craft, and violence? a God to whom, perhaps not even the rapturous *ardeurs* of triumph and annihilation would be known? People would not understand such a God: why should they have him?—To be sure, when a people goes to ruin; when it feels its belief in the future, and its hope of freedom finally vanish; when it becomes conscious of submission as the first utility, and of the virtues of the submissive as conditions of maintenance, then its God also is obliged to change. He now becomes a sneak, timid and modest, he counsels "peace of soul," an end of hatred, indulgence, "love" even towards friend and foe. He constantly moralises, he creeps into the cave of every private virtue, he becomes everybody's God, he becomes a private man, he becomes a cosmopolitan. Formerly, he represented a people, the strength of a people, all that was aggressive and thirsty for power in the soul of a people; now he is merely the good God . . . In fact, there is no other alternative for Gods; they are *either* the will to power—and so long they will be national Gods,—*or* else the impotence to power—and then they necessarily become *good* . . .

17

Wherever the will to power declines in any way, there is always also a physiological retrogression, a *décadence*. The Deity of *décadence*, pruned of his manliest virtues and impulses, henceforth becomes necessarily the God of the physiologically retrograde, the weak. They do not call themselves the weak, they call themselves the "good" . . . It is obvious (without a further hint being necessary) in what moments in history, only, the dualistic fiction of a good and a bad God became possible. Through the same instinct by which the subjugated lower their God to the "good in itself," they obliterate the good qualities out of the God of their conquerors; they take revenge on their masters by *bedevilling* their God.—The *good* God, just like the devil: both are abortions of *décadence*.—How can one still defer so much to the simplicity of Christian theologians, as to decree with them that the continuous development of the concept of God from the "God of Israel," from the national God to the Christian God, to the essence of everything good, is a *progress?* — But so does even Renan. As if Renan had a right to simplicity! It is just the very opposite that strikes the eye. When the presuppositions of *ascending* life, when everything strong, brave, domineering, and proud have been eliminated out of the concept of God, when he sinks step by step to the symbol of a staff for the fatigued, a sheet-anchor for all drowning ones, when he becomes poor people's God, sinners' God, the God of the sick *par excellence,* and when the predicate of Saviour, Redeemer, is left as the sole divine predicate: *what* does such a change speak of? such a *reduction* of the Divine? — To be sure, the kingdom of God has thereby become greater. Formerly, he had only his people, his "chosen" people. Since then he has gone abroad on his travels, quite like his people itself, since then he has never again settled down quietly in any place: until he has finally become at home everywhere, the great cosmopolitan, — till he has gained over the "great number," and the half of earth to his side. But the God of the "great number," the democrat among Gods, became, nevertheless, no proud pagan God: he remained a Jew, he remained the God of the nooks, the God of all dark corners and places, of all unhealthy quarters throughout the world! . . . His world empire is still, as formerly, an under-world empire, a hospital, a subterranean empire, a Ghetto empire . . . And he himself so pale, so weak, so *décadent* . . . Even the palest of the pale still became master over him, — Messrs. the metaphysicians, the conceptual albinos. They spun round about him so long, until, hypnotised by their movements, he became a cobweb-spinner, a metaphysician himself. Henceforth he spun the world anew out of himself, — *sub specie Spinozæ,* — henceforth he transfigured himself always into the thinner and the paler, he became "ideal," he became "pure spirit," he became "*absolutum,*" he became "thing in itself" . . . *Ruin of a God:* God became "thing in itself" . . .

18

The Christian concept of God — God as God of the sick, God as cobweb-spinner, God as spirit — is one of the most corrupt concepts of God ever arrived at on earth; it represents perhaps the gauge of low water in the descending development of the God-type. God degenerated to the *contradiction of life,* instead of being its transfiguration and its eternal *yea!* In God, hostility announced to life, to nature, to the will to life! God as the formula for every calumny of "this world," for every lie of "another world!" In God nothingness deified, the will to nothingness declared holy! . . .

19

That the strong races of Northern Europe have not thrust from themselves the Christian God, is verily no honour to their religious talent,
not to speak of their taste. They ought to have got the better of such a
sickly and decrepit product of *décadence*. There lies a curse upon
them, because they have not got the better of it: they have incorporated
sickness, old age and contradiction into all their instincts,—they have
created no God since! Two millenniums almost, and not a single new
God! But still continuing, and as if persisting by right, as an *ultimatum*
and *maximum* of the God-shaping force, of the *creator spiritus* in man,
this pitiable God of Christian monotono-theism! This hybrid image of
ruin, derived from nullity, concept and contradiction in which all
décadence instincts, all cowardices and lassitudes of soul have their
sanction!

20

With my condemnation of Christianity, I should not like to have done
an injustice to a kindred religion, which even preponderates in the
number of its followers,—to *Buddhism*. The two are related as nihilistic religions—they are *décadence*-religions,—both are separated from
one another in the most remarkable manner. For the fact that they can
now be *compared* the critic of Christianity is profoundly grateful to the
Indian scholars.—Buddhism is a hundred times more realistic than
Christianity,—it has in its nature the heritage of an objective and cool
propounding of questions, it arrives *after* a philosophical movement
lasting hundreds of years; the concept of "God" is already done away
with when it arrives. Buddhism is the only properly *positivist* religion
which history shows us, even in its theory of perception (a strict phe-
nomenalism)—it no longer speaks of a "struggle against *sin*," but, quite
doing justice to actuality, it speaks of a "struggle against *suffering*." It
has—this distinguishes it profoundly from Christianity—the self-
deception of moral concepts behind it—it stands, in my language, *beyond* good and evil.—The two physiological facts on which it rests and
which it has in view are, on the one hand, an excessive excitableness of
sensibility, which expresses itself as a refined capacity for pain, and, on
the other hand, an over-intellectualising, an over-long occupation with
concepts and logical procedures through which the personal instinct
has received damage to the advantage of the "impersonal." (Both are
conditions, which at least some of my readers, the "objective," will
know, like myself, by experience.) On the basis of these physiological
conditions a *depression* has originated: against which Buddha takes hy-
gienic measures. He applies life in the open air as a measure against it,

wandering life; moderation and selection in food; precaution against all intoxicants; similarly precautions against all emotions which create bile, or heat the blood; no *anxiety* either for self or for others. He requires notions which either give repose or gaiety,—he devises means to disaccustom one's self from others. He understands goodness, benignity, as health-promoting. *Prayer* is excluded like *asceticism*; no categorical imperative, no *compulsion* at all, not even within the monastic community (a person can leave it). These would all be means to strengthen that excessive excitableness. Just on that account he does not require either a struggle against those who think differently; his doctrine resists nothing *so much* as the feeling of revenge, of aversion, of *resentment* ("hostility does not come to an end by hostility:" the moving refrain of the whole of Buddhism . . .). And rightly so: these very emotions would be extremely *insalutary* in respect to the main regiminal purpose. The intellectual fatigue which he lights upon, and which is expressed in an over-great "objectivity" (that is, weakening of individual interest, loss of weight, of egotism), he combats by strictly reconducting even the most intellectual interests back to the *individual*. In the doctrine of Buddha egotism became duty: the "one thing needful," the "how art *thou* freed from suffering," regulated and determined the whole intellectual regimen—(one may perhaps call to one's mind that Athenian who likewise waged war against pure "scientificness," Socrates, who elevated personal egotism to morality even in the domain of problems).

21

The pre-requisite for Buddhism is a very mild climate, great gentleness and liberality in usages, *no* militarism,—and that it is the higher and learned classes in whom the movement has its focus. Cheerfulness, tranquillity, and non-desire are wanted as the highest goal, and the goal is *attained*. Buddhism is not a religion in which perfection is merely aspired after: the perfect is the normal case.—

In Christianity the instincts of the subjugated and suppressed come into the foreground: it is the lowest classes who here seek their goal. Here the casuistry of sin, self-criticism and inquisition of conscience are practised as occupations, as expedients against irksomeness; here the emotion towards a *powerful one*, called "God," is constantly maintained (by prayer); here the highest is regarded as unattainable, as a gift, as "grace." Here also publicity is lacking: the hiding-place, the dark chamber are Christian. Here the body is despised, hygiene is repudiated as sensuousness; the Church resists even cleanliness (the first Christian regulation, after the expulsion of the Moors, was the closing of the public baths, of which Cordova alone possessed 270). A certain sense of cruelty towards self and others is Christian; the hatred against those thinking differently; the will to persecute. Gloomy and exciting concepts are in the foreground; the most greatly coveted states, designated with the highest names, are epileptoid states; the regimen is so chosen that it favours morbid phenomena and over-excites the *nerves*. The deadly hostility against the lords of the earth, the "noble"—and at the same time a concealed, secret competition with them (one leaves them the "*body*," one *only* wants the "soul")—are Christian. The hatred of *intellect*, of pride, courage, freedom, *libertinage* of intellect, is Christian: the hatred of the *senses*, of the delights of the senses, of all delight, is Christian . . .

22

Christianity, when it left its first soil, the lowest classes, the *underworld* of the ancient world, when it went abroad among the barbarian nations in quest of power, had no longer to presuppose *fatigued* men, but internally savage, self-lacerating men—strong but ill-constituted men. The discontentedness of man with himself, the suffering from himself, is *not* here an excessive excitableness and capacity for pain, as it is in the case of Buddhists; but reversely is an over-powerful longing for *causing pain*, for discharging the inner tension in hostile actions and concepts. Christianity had need of *barbarous* notions and values in order to become master of barbarians; such are the sacrifice of firstlings, the blood-drinking at the communion, the contempt of intellect and of culture; torture in all its forms corporeal and incorporeal; the great pomp of worship. Buddhism is a religion for *late* men, for kind, gentle races who have become over-intellectual and feel pain too readily (Europe is as yet far from being ripe for it): it is a conveyance of them back to peace and cheerfulness, to regimen in intellectual matters, to a certain hardening in corporeal matters. Christianity desires to become master of *beasts of prey*; its expedient is to make them sick—weakening is the Christian recipe for *taming*, for "civilisation." Buddhism is a religion for the close and the worn-out-ness of civilisation which Christianity does not as yet find in existence—but which it may establish under certain conditions.

23

Buddhism, to repeat once more, is a hundred times colder, sincerer, and more objective. It no longer needs to make its suffering, its capacity for pain, *decent* by the interpretation of sin,—it says simply what it thinks, "I suffer." For the barbarian, on the contrary, suffering in itself is no decent thing: he needs first an explanation in order to confess to himself *that* he suffers (his instinct points him rather to the denial of suffering, to silent endurance). Here the word "devil" was a God-send: people had an over-powerful and terrible enemy,—they did not need to be ashamed of suffering from such an enemy.—

Christianity has some refinements at its basis which belong to the Orient. Above all, Christianity knows that it is quite indifferent if aught is true, but of the highest importance *so far as* it is believed to be true. Truth, and the *belief* that aught is true: two worlds with entirely exclusive interests, almost *antithetical* worlds,—one arrives at each of the two by fundamentally different paths. To be aware of this, *makes* almost a wise man in the Orient: it is thus that Brahmans understand it, it is thus that Plato understands it, it is thus that every scholar of esoteric wisdom understands it. When, for example, it is a *happiness* for a person to believe himself saved from sin, it is *not* necessary, as a pre-requisite thereto, that he be sinful, but only that he *feel* himself sinful. When, however, *belief* is necessary above everything else, reason, perception, and investigation must be brought into discredit: the way to truth becomes a *forbidden* way.—Strong *hope* is a far greater stimulus to life than any single, actually occurring happiness. Sufferers must be maintained by a hope which cannot be contradicted by any actuality,—which is not *done away with* by a fulfilment: an other-world hope. (Just on account of this capability of keeping the unfortunate person in suspense, hope was regarded among the Greeks as the evil of evils, as the peculiarly *insidious* evil: it remained behind in the box of evil.)—In order that *love* may be possible, God must be a person; in order that the lowest instincts may have a voice, God must be young. It is necessary for the fervour of women to move a handsome saint into the foreground, for the fervour of men a Maria. This, of course, on the presupposition that Christianity desires to become master on a soil where Aphrodisian or Adonis worships have already determined the *concept* of worship. The requirement of *chastity* strengthens the vehemence and internality of religious instinct—it makes worship warmer, more enthusiastic, more soul-breathing.—Love is the state in which man sees things most widely *different* from what they are. Illusory power is there at its height, like sweetening and *transfiguring* power. One endures more in love than at other times, one puts up with everything. The problem was to devise a religion in which it was possible to love: with that one is beyond the worst ills of life—one no longer sees them.—So much concerning the three Christian virtues, faith, charity, and hope: I call them the three Christian shrewdnesses.—Buddhism is too late, too positivist to be still shrewd in this manner.—

24

I only touch here on the problem of the *origin* of Christianity. The *first* sentence for its solution is: Christianity can only be understood if one understands the soil out of which it has grown,—it is *not* a countermovement to Jewish instinct, it is rather the logical consequence of it, a further inference in its awe-inspiring logic. In the formula of the Redeemer: "salvation is of the Jews."—The *second* principle: the psychological type of the Galilean is still recognisable, but only in its complete degeneration (which at the same time is mutilation and an overloading with foreign traits) could it serve the purpose for which it has been used, to be the type of a *Redeemer* of mankind.—

The Jews are the most remarkable people in the history of the world, because, when confronted with the question of being or not being, they preferred, with a perfectly weird consciousness, being *at any price*: this price was the radical *falsifying* of all nature, of all naturalness, of all actuality, of the entire inner world as well as the outer. They demarcated their position counter to all conditions under which hitherto a people could live, *was permitted* to live; they created out of themselves a concept antithetical to the *natural* conditions,—they successively reversed, in an irreparable manner, religion, worship, morality, history, and psychology, *into the contradiction of their natural values*. We meet with the same phenomenon once more, and in ineffably magnified proportions, although only as a copy:—the Christian Church, in comparison with the "saintly people," dispenses with all pretensions to originality. The Jews, just on that account, are the most *fatal* nation in the history of the world: in their after-effect they made mankind false to such an extent that a Christian can even at present cherish an anti-Jewish feeling without comprehending that he is the *ultimate consequence of Judaism*.

I have brought forward psychologically for the first time, in my "Genealogy of Morals," the antithetical concepts of a noble morality and of a *ressentiment* morality, the latter originated *out of a negation* of the former: but this is Jewish-Christian morality wholly and entirely. To be able to negative all that represents the *ascending* movement of life on earth, well-constitutedness, power, beauty, self-affirmation, the instinct of *ressentiment*, developed to genius, had here to devise for itself *another* world, from which the *affirmation of life* appeared as the evil, as the repudiable in itself. Psychologically re-examined, the Jewish people is a people of the toughest vital force. Placed under impossible conditions, voluntarily, out of a most profound policy of self-maintenance, it took the part of all *décadence* instincts,—not as ruled by them, but because it divined in them a power by which to get along *in opposition to* "the world." They are the counterpart of all *décadents*: they were compelled to *exhibit* them to illusion, they have, with a *non plus ultra* of theatrical genius, known how to place themselves at the head of all *décadence* movements (as the Christianity of *Paul*), and have created something out of them which is stronger than any party *affirmative* of life. *Décadence*, for the class of men who aspired to power in Judaism and Christianity (a *priestly* class), is but a *means*; this class of men has a vital interest in making mankind *sick*, and in reversing the concepts "good" and "bad," "true" and "false" into a mortally dangerous and world-calumniating signification.

25

The history of Israel is invaluable as a typical history of the *denaturalising* of natural values; I indicate five matters of fact in this process. Originally, and above all in the time of the kingdom, Israel like other people stood in the *right* relation, *i.e.* in the natural relation to all things. Their Javeh was the expression of consciousness of power, the delight in themselves, the hope of themselves: in him they expected victory and prosperity, with him they had confidence in nature, that it would furnish what they needed—above all rain. Javeh is the God of Israel, and *consequently* the God of justice: the logic of every people that is in power and has a good conscience thereof. In the festal worship both these sides of self-affirmation of a people are expressed: it is thankful for the great destinies by which it came to the fore; it is thankful in relation to the course of the year and all the good fortune in cattle-rearing and agriculture.—This state of things continued for a long time the ideal, even when, in a sad manner, it was done away with: anarchy within and the Assyrian from without. But the people firmly retained, as their highest desirability, the vision of a king who was a good soldier and a strict judge: above all that typical prophet (*i.e.* critic and satirist of the hour), Isaiah.—But every hope remained unrealised. The old God *could* no longer do what he formerly could. They might have to let him go. What happened? They *changed* his concept,—they *denaturalised* his concept: they held him fast at that price.—Javeh, the God of "justice,"—*no longer* a unity with Israel, an expression of national pride: only a God under conditions . . . The concept of God becomes an instrument in the hands of priestly agitators, who henceforth interpret all good fortune as reward, all misfortune as punishment for disobedience to God, for "sin:" that most falsified manner of interpretation of a pretended "moral order of the world" with which, once for all, the natural concepts of "cause" and "effect" are turned upside down. As soon as natural causality by means of reward and punishment has been done away with, an *antinatural* causality is needed: all the rest of antinaturalness then follows. A God who demands,—in place of a God who helps, who surmounts difficulties, who is, after all, the word for every happy inspiration of courage and self-confidence . . . *Morality*, no longer the expression of the conditions of the life and growth of a people, no longer its fundamental instinct of life, but become abstract, the antithesis of life,— Morality as a fundamental debasement of phantasy, as "evil eye" for everything. *What* is Jewish, *what* is Christian morality? Chance despoiled of its innocence; misfortune befouled with the concept of "sin;" well-being as danger, as "temptation;" bad physiological condition poisoned by the serpent of conscience . . .

26

The concept of God falsified; the concept of morality falsified:—the Jewish priesthood did not remain at rest there. They could make no use of the whole *history* of Israel: away with it!—These priests brought about that miracle of falsification the document of which lies before us in a good part of the Bible: with an unequalled scorn of every tradition, of every historical reality, they translated the past of their own people *into the religious*; that is, they made out of it a stupid salvation-mechanism of offence against Javeh and punishment, of piety towards Javeh and reward. We would feel this most disgraceful act of historical falsification much more painfully, if the *ecclesiastical* interpretation of the history of millenniums had not almost blunted us to the requirement of uprightness *in historicis*. And the philosophers seconded the Church: *the lie* of "a moral order of the world" goes through the whole development even of modern philosophy. What does "moral order of the world" signify? That there is once for all a will of God, as to what men have to do and what they have not to do; that the value of a people, or of an individual, is determined by how much or how little the will of God is obeyed; that in the destinies of a people, or of an individual, the will of God is demonstrated as *ruling; i.e.* as punishing and rewarding in proportion to obedience. The *reality* in place of this pitiable lie is that a parasitic species of man, the priests, who only flourish at the cost of all sound formations of life, misuse the name of God: they call a condition of things in which the priest determines the value of things, "the kingdom of God;" they call the means by which such a condition is attained or maintained "the will of God;" with a cold-blooded cynicism, they estimate people, ages, and individuals, according as they were serviceable to the priestly ascendency, or resisted it.

Let us see them at work: under the hands of Jewish priests the *great* period in the history of Israel became a period of decay; the exile, the long misfortune was transformed into an eternal *punishment* for the great period—a period in which as yet the priest was nothing. According to their requirement, they made miserable sneaking creatures and hypocrites, or "ungodly" persons out of the powerful and *very freely* constituted characters in the history of Israel, they simplified the psychology of every great event into the idiotic formula, "obedience *or* disobedience to God."—A step further: "the will of God," *i.e.* the conditions of maintenance for the power of the priest, must be *known*,—for this purpose a "revelation" is needed. *I.e.* a great literary forgery becomes necessary, a "holy book" is discovered,—it is made public with all hieratic pomp, with fast-days and cries of lamentation for the long "sin." The "will of God" was fixed for ever so long, the whole evil lay in the fact that people had estranged themselves from the "holy book" . . . Moses was already the revealed "will of God" . . . What had happened? The priest, with severity and with pedantry, had once for all formulated *what he wanted to have,* "what is the will of God," even to the great and the small imposts which had to be paid to him (not to forget the most savoury pieces of flesh, for the priest is a beefsteak eater) . . . From henceforth all the affairs of life are so regulated that the priest is *everywhere indispensable*; at all natural events of life, at birth, at marriage, in sickness, at death, not to speak of the sacrifice (the meal), the holy parasite appears, in order to *denaturalise* them; in his language, to "sanctify" them . . . For that must be comprehended: every natural custom, every natural institution (the state, the administration of justice, marriage, the care of the sick and the poor), every requirement prompted by the instinct of life, everything, in short, that has its value *in itself* is, as a principle, made worthless, *inimical* to any value, by the parasitism of the priest (or of a moral order of the world),—it has need of a supplementary sanction, a *value-bestowing* power is necessary, which denies naturalness therein, which just thereby *creates* value. The priest depreciates, *desecrates* naturalness: it is only at this cost that he exists at all.—Disobedience to God, *i.e.* to the priest, to "law" now gets the name of "sin;" the means for a person "reconciling him again to God," as is only fair, are means by which the subjugation under the priest is only more thoroughly guaranteed: the priest alone "saves" . . . Re-examined psychologically, "sins" are indispensable in every society priestly-organised: they are the real handles of power, the priest *lives* by the sins, it is needful for him that there should be sinning . . . Principal proposition: "God forgives him who does penance," *i.e. him who submits himself to the priest.*—

27

On a soil, *falsified* to that extent where all naturalness, every natural value, all *reality*, had the profoundest instincts of the ruling class opposed to it, *Christianity* grew up, a form of mortal hostility to reality which has not hitherto been surpassed. The "holy people" who had maintained only priestly values, only priestly words, for all matters, and who, with a logicalness of conclusion which may inspire awe, had separated from themselves everything of power besides that existed on earth, as from the "unholy," "the world," "sin," — this people produced for its instinct a final formula which was logical to the point of self-negation: as *Christianity*, it negatived even the last form of reality, the "holy people," the "chosen people," *Jewish* reality itself. The case is of the first rank: the small seditious movement which is christened by the name of Jesus of Nazareth, is the Jewish instinct *once more*, —expressed in other terms, the priestly instinct, which no longer endures the priest as a reality, the invention of a yet *more abstract* form of existence, a yet more *unreal* vision of the world, than is determined by the organisation of a Church. Christianity *negatives* the Church . . .

I fail to see what the uprising was directed against, as the originator of which Jesus has been understood or *misunderstood*, if it was not an uprising against the Jewish Church, the word "church" taken precisely in the sense in which we at present take it. It was an uprising against the "good and just," against "the saints of Israel," against the hierarchy of society—*not* against its corruption but against caste, privilege, order, formula, it was the *unbelief* in "higher men," the denial of all that was priest and theologian. But the hierarchy which was thereby, though but for an instant, called in question, was the pile-work on which alone the Jewish people continued in the midst of the "waters," the toilsomely acquired *last* possibility of being left, the *residuum* of its detached political existence; an attack upon it was an attack upon the profoundest national instinct, upon the toughest national will to life which has ever existed on earth. This holy anarchist who incited the lowest class, the outcasts and "sinners," the *Chandalas* within Judaism, to opposition against the ruling order (with language which, if the Gospels can be trusted, would even at the present day send a person to Siberia), was a political criminal, so far as political criminals were possible in an *absurdly unpolitical* community. This brought him to the cross: the proof of it is the inscription on the cross. He died for *his* guilt, —all ground is lacking for the assertion, however often it has been made, that he died for the guilt of others. —

28

It is quite another question whether he was at all conscious of a contrast of that kind, whether he was not merely left to be such a contrast. And it is but here that I touch on the problem of the *psychology of the Saviour.*

—I confess that I read few books with such difficulties as the Gospels. These difficulties are other than those in whose indication the learned curiosity of German intellect has celebrated one of its most memorable triumphs. The time is far distant when I with the sage dulness of a refined philologist, like every young scholar, tasted thoroughly the work of incomparable Strauss. I was then twenty years of age: I am now too serious for that. Of what account are the contradictions of "tradition" to me? How can legends of saints be called "tradition" at all? The stories of saints are the most ambiguous literature that exists: to apply scientific methods to it *when no documents besides have reached us,* appears to me condemned in principle—mere learned idling.

29

What is of account to *me* is the psychological type of the Saviour. For it *might* be contained in the Gospels, in spite of the Gospels, however much it might be mutilated or overloaded with strange features: as that of Francis of Assisi is contained in his legends, in spite of the legends. *Not* the truth with regard to what he did or said, or how he died exactly; but the question *whether* his type is at all representable now, whether it is "handed down" to us. The attempts with which I am acquainted to pick out of the Gospels even the *history* of a soul, seem to me to be proofs of a detestable psychological frivolity. M. Renan, a buffoon *in psychologicis,* got the two most *inappropriate* concepts imaginable into his explanation of the type of Jesus, the concept of *genius* and the concept of *hero* ("*héros*"). But if anything be unevangelical it is the concept of hero. Just the antithesis to all contending, to all feeling one's self in struggle has here become instinct, the incapacity for resistance here becomes morality ("resist not evil:" the profoundest saying of the Gospels; in a certain sense, the key to them), blessedness in peace, in gentleness, in *inability* to be hostile. What is "glad tidings?" True life, eternal life has been found—it is not promised, it is there, it is *in you:* as life in love, in love without abatement, and exemption, without distance. Everyone is the child of God—Jesus does not at all claim anything for himself alone,—as a child of God everyone is equal to everyone else ... To make a *hero* out of Jesus!—and to think what a misunderstanding is the word "genius!" Our whole concept of "intellect," our cultured concept of it, has no meaning at all in the world in which Jesus lived. If one would speak with the rigidity of the physiologist, quite another word would be the thing here . . . We know a condition of morbid excitability of the *sense of touch* in which the latter shrinks back in horror from every contact, from every seizing of a firm object. Let such a physiological *habitus* be translated into its ultimate logic — as an instinctive hatred against *every* reality; as a flight into the "unintelligible," into the "incomprehensible;" as an aversion from every formula, every concept of time and space, against all that is firmly established, custom, institution, church; as feeling at home in a world with which no mode of reality is any longer in touch, in a merely "inner" world, a "true" world, an "eternal" world . . . "The kingdom of God is *within you*" . . .

30

The instinctive hatred of reality: consequence of an extreme liability to suffering and excitement, which no longer wants to be "touched" at all, because it feels all contact too profoundly.

The instinctive exclusion of all antipathy, of all hostility, of all sentiment of limits and distances: consequence of an extreme liability to suffering and excitement, which feels every resistance on its own part, every necessity for resistance as an intolerable *displeasure* (*i.e.* as *injurious*, as *dissuaded* by self-preservative instinct), and which knows blessedness (delight) only in no longer offering opposition, to anyone either to the ill or to the evil, — love as sole, as final possibility of life . . .

These are the two *physiological realities* upon which, out of which the salvation doctrine has grown. I call them a sublime, extended development of Hedonism on a thoroughly morbid basis. Although with a large addition of Greek vitality and nerve force, Epicurism, the salvation doctrine of Paganism, remains most closely related to it. Epicurus, a *typical décadent*: first recognised by me as such. — The fear of pain, even of the infinitely small in pain, — it cannot end otherwise than as a *religion of love* . . .

31

I have given beforehand my answer to the problem. The pre-requisite for it is that the type of the Saviour be but preserved to us in a strong distortion. This distortion has in itself much probability: such a type could not for several reasons remain pure, entire, or free from additions. The *milieu* in which this strange character moved must have made its marks upon it, as the history, the *fate* of the first Christian community must have done still more: by that fate the type was reciprocally enriched with traits which only become comprehensible by warfare, and by the purposes of propaganda. By that strange and sickly world into which we are introduced by the Gospels—a world as if taken from a Russian novel in which the outcasts of society, nervous affections and childish idiotism, seem to have appointed a *rendezvous*—the type must under all circumstances have been *rendered coarser*; the first disciples especially translated an essence swimming entirely in symbols and incomprehensibilities into their own crudity in order to understand anything of it at all,—for them the type was only *existent* after having been pressed into better-known forms . . . The prophet, the Messiah, the future judge, the moral teacher, the thaumaturgist, John the Baptist—just so many opportunities for mistaking the type . . . Finally let us not undervalue the *proprium* of all great veneration, especially sectarian veneration; it extinguishes the original and often painfully alien characteristics and idiosyncrasies in the venerated being—*it does not see them itself.* One has to regret that a Dostoiewsky has not lived in the neighbourhood of this most interesting *décadent,* I mean someone who knew just how to perceive the thrilling charm of such a mixture of the sublime, the sickly, and the childish. A last point of view: the type, as a *décadence* type, could actually have been of a peculiar plurality and contradictoriness: such a possibility is not completely to be excluded. Nevertheless everything dissuades therefrom: tradition above all would have to be remarkably true and objective in this case, of which we have reasons for supposing the contrary. In the meanwhile there yawns a contradiction between the mountain, lake, and meadow preacher (whose appearance impresses one like that of a Buddha on a soil very unlike that of India), and the fanatical aggressor, the deadly enemy of theologians and priests, whom Renan's malice has glorified as *le grand maître en ironie.* I myself do not doubt that the profuse amount of gall (and even of *esprit*) has only overflowed upon the type of the master out of the excited condition of Christian propaganda: one knows well the unhesitatingness of all sectaries to shape their master into an *apology* of themselves. When the first community had need of a censuring, wrangling, wrathful, maliciously subtle theologian *in opposition to* theologians, they created their God according to their need: as they also, without hesitation, put into his mouth those completely unevangelical concepts which they could not then do without—the "second coming," the "last judgment," every kind of temporal expectation and promise.—

32

I resist, let it be said once more, the introducing of the fanatic into the type of the Saviour: the very word *impérieux* which Renan used *annulled* the type. The "good tidings" are just that there are no more antitheses; the kingdom of heaven belongs to *children*; the faith whose voice is heard here is not a faith acquired by struggle,—it is there, it is from the beginning, it is, as it were, a childlikeness which has flowed back into the intellectual. The case of retarded puberty undeveloped in the organism, as a phenomenon resulting from degeneration, is at least familiar to physiologists.—Such a belief is not angry, it does not find fault, it does not offer resistance; it does not bring "the sword," it has no idea in what respect it might some day separate people. It does not prove itself either by miracles or by reward and promise, or even "by the Scripture:" it is every moment its own miracle, its own reward, its own proof, its own "kingdom of God." Neither does this belief formulate itself—it *lives*, it resists formulæ. To be sure, the accident of environment, of language, of schooling, determines a certain circle of concepts: primitive Christianity uses *only* Jewish-Semitic concepts (the eating and drinking at the communion belong here, those concepts, so badly misused by the Church, like everything Jewish). But let us be careful not to see therein anything more than a symbolic speech, a semeiotic, an opportunity for similes. It is precisely the preliminary condition of this anti-realist being able to speak at all, that not a single word is taken literally. Among the Indians, he would have made use of the Sankhyam concepts; among the Chinese, he would have made use of those of Laotse—and would have felt no difference thereby.—One might, with some tolerance of expression, call Jesus a "free spirit"—he does not care a bit for anything fixed: the word *killeth*, all that is fixed *killeth*. The concept, the *experience* of "life" as he alone knows it is with him repugnant to every kind of expression, formula, law, belief, or dogma. He speaks merely of the inmost things: "life," or "truth," or "light," are his expressions for the inmost things,—everything else, the whole of reality, the whole of nature, language itself, has for him merely the value of a sign, or a simile.—Here, one must take care not to mistake anything, however great the seduction may be which lies in Christian, *i.e.* in *ecclesiastical* prejudice. Such a symbolism *par excellence* stands outside of all religion, all concepts of worship, all history, all natural science, all experience of the world, all knowledge, all politics, all psychology, all books, all art—the "knowledge" of Jesus is just the *pure folly that* there should be anything of that kind. *Civilisation* is not even known to him by hearsay, he has no need of any struggle against it—he does not negative it. The same is true of the *state*, of the whole civil order and society, of *labour*, of war; he has never had any reason to negative the "world," he has never had any idea of the ecclesiastical concept of the "world." *Negation* is just what is quite impossible for him.—Dialectics is similarly lacking, it lacks the notion that a belief, a "truth," could be proved by reasons (*his* proofs are internal "lights," internal feelings of delight, and self-affirmations, nothing but "proofs of force"). Such a doctrine is not even *able* to contradict, it does not even conceive that there are other doctrines, that there *can be* other doctrines, it does not even know how to represent to itself an opposite mode of thinking . . . *Where* such is met with, the former will mourn concerning "blindness" from heartiest sympathy—for it sees the "light,"—but it will make no objection . . .

33

In the entire psychology of the gospel the concepts of guilt and punishment are lacking; similarly the concept of reward. "Sin," every relation of distance between God and man, is done away with,—*it is just that which is the "glad tidings."* Blessedness is not promised, it does not depend on conditions: it is the *sole* reality—the rest is symbolism for speaking of it.

The *consequence* of such a condition projects itself into a new *practice*, the truly evangelical practice. It is not a "belief" which distinguishes the Christian: the Christian acts, he distinguishes himself by *another* mode of acting. In that he does not offer resistance either by word or in heart to those acting in a hostile way towards him. In that he makes no distinction between foreigners and natives, between Jews and not-Jews (the neighbour, properly, the fellow-believer, the Jew). In that he does not get angry at anyone, does not despise anyone. In that he neither lets himself be seen in the law-courts, nor takes their claims into account ("not swearing"). In that, under no circumstances, does he separate from his wife, not even in the case of her proved unfaithfulness.—All fundamentally one proposition, all the consequences of one instinct.—

The life of the Saviour was nothing else but *this* practice,—neither was his death anything else . . . He had no need of any formulæ or rites for intercourse with God—not even of prayer. He has settled accounts with the whole of the Jewish expiation and reconciliation doctrine; he knows that it is by the *practice* of life alone that one feels himself "divine," "blessed," "evangelical," at all times a "child of God." *Neither* "penitence," *nor* "prayer for forgiveness" is a way to God: *evangelical practice alone* leads to God, *is* itself "God."—What was abolished by the gospel, was the Judaism of the concepts of "sin," "forgiveness of sin," "faith," "salvation by faith,"—the entire Jewish ecclesiastical doctrine was negatived in the "glad tidings."

The profound instinct for the problem how to *live* in order to feel one's self "in heaven," to feel one's self "eternal," while in every other relation one feels that one is *not in the least* "in heaven:" this alone is the psychological reality of "salvation."—A new mode of conduct, *not a new faith* . . .

34

If I understand anything of this great symbolist, it is that he only took *inner* realities as realities, as "truths,"—that he only understood the rest, all that is natural, temporal, spatial, historical, as signs, as occasion for similes. The concept of the "Son of Man," is not a concrete person belonging to history, some individual, solitary case, but an "eternal" fact, a psychological symbol freed from the concept of time. The same is again true, and true in the highest sense, of the *God* of this typical symbolist, of the "kingdom of God," of the "kingdom of heaven," the "sonship of God." Nothing is more un-Christian than the *ecclesiastical crudities* of a God as a *person*, of a "kingdom of God" which *comes*, of a "kingdom of heaven" *in another world*, of a "Son of God," the *second person* of the Trinity. All that is—forgive me the expression—the *fist* in the eye (oh, in what sort of an eye!) of the gospel: *historical cynicism* in the mockery of the symbol . . . But it is quite palpable what is touched upon by the figures of "father" and "son" (not palpable for everyone, I admit): by the word "son" the *entrance* into the collective sentiment of transfiguration of all things (blessedness) is expressed; by the word "father," *this sentiment itself*, the sentiment of eternalness and completeness.—I am ashamed to call to mind what the Church has made out of this symbolism: has it not placed an Amphitryon story at the threshold of Christian "faith?" And a dogma of immaculate conception over and above . . . *But it has thereby maculated conception.*——

The "kingdom of heaven" is a state of the heart—not something which comes "over the earth" or "after death." The entire concept of natural death *is lacking* in the gospel: death is no bridge, no transition; the concept is lacking, because it belongs to an entirely different world, which is merely apparent, merely useful to serve for symbolism. The "hour of death" is *no* Christian concept,—the "hour," time, physical life and its crises, do not at all exist for the teacher of the "glad tidings" . . . The "kingdom of God" is nothing which is expected, it has no yesterday and no day after to-morrow, it does not come in a "thousand years"—it is an experience in a heart; it is everywhere present, it is nowhere present . . .

35

This "bringer of glad tidings" died as he lived, as he *taught*—not "to save men," but to show how one ought to live. It is the *practice* which he left behind to mankind, his behaviour before the judges, before the lictors, before his accusers, and in presence of every kind of calumny and mockery—his behaviour on the *cross*. He does not resist, he does not defend his right, he takes no step to avert from himself the extremest consequences; yet more, *he exacts them* . . . And he entreats, he suffers, he loves—with those, *in* those who do him wrong . . . *Not* to defend himself, *not* to be angry, *not* to make answerable . . . But not even to resist an evil one,—to *love* him . . .

36

—Only we, we *emancipated* spirits, have the pre-requisite for understanding a thing which has been misunderstood by nineteen centuries,—that uprightness, become instinctive and passionate, which makes war against the holy lie even more than against any other . . . People were unspeakably far from our affectionate and prudent neutrality, from that discipline of intellect which alone makes it possible to find out such unfamiliar and delicate affairs: with an insolent selfishness, they always sought only *their own* advantage therein, they erected the *Church* out of the antithesis to the gospel . . .

He who sought for signs that an ironical Divinity operated behind the great drama of the world, would find no small support in the *stupendous question-mark* called Christianity. That mankind should bow the knee before the antithesis of that which was the origin, the meaning and the *right* of the gospel, that they should have declared holy precisely those features in the concept of "Church" which the "bringer of glad tidings" regarded as *beneath* him, as *behind* him—one would seek in vain for a grander form of *grand historical irony*.——

37

Our age is proud of its historical sense: how has it been able to make itself believe in the absurdity that the *gross thaumaturgist and redeemer fable* stands at the commencement of Christianity,—and that everything spiritual and symbolic is only a later development? Reversely: the history of Christianity—and, of course, from the death on the cross onwards—is the history of the gradually grosser and grosser misunderstanding of an *original* symbolism. With every extension of Christianity over still broader, still ruder masses in whom the pre-requisites out of which it was born were more and more lacking, it became more necessary to *vulgarise*, to *barbarise* Christianity,—it has taken into itself doctrines and rites from all the *subterranean* cults of the *imperium Romanum*, and the absurdity of all kinds of sickly reason. The fate of Christianity lay in the necessity that its faith itself had to become as sickly, as low and vulgar as the needs were sickly, low, and vulgar which had to be gratified by it. As Church the sickly barbarism itself finally swells up into power,—Church, that form of deadly hostility to all uprightness, to all *elevation* of soul, to all discipline of intellect, to all ingenious and gracious humanity.—The *Christian*—the *noble* values: it is only we, we *emancipated* spirits, who have re-established this greatest of all antitheses of values!—

38

I do not suppress a sigh at this place. There are days when I am visited by a feeling, blacker than the blackest melancholy—*contempt of man.* And that I may leave no doubt with regard to *what* I despise, *whom* I despise,—it is the man of to-day, the man with whom I am fatally contemporaneous. The man of to-day—I suffocate from his impure breath . . . With respect to what is past, I am, like all who perceive, of a great tolerance, *i.e.* a *generous* self-overcoming. With a gloomy circumspection I go through the madhouse world of entire millenniums (it may be called "Christianity," "Christian faith," "Christian Church"),—I take care not to make mankind accountable for its insanities. But my feeling changes suddenly, and breaks out as soon as I enter the modern period, *our* period. Our age *knows* . . . What was formerly merely morbid, now has become unseemly,—it is now unseemly to be a Christian. *And here my loathing commences.*—I look around me: there is no longer a word left of what was formerly called "truth," we no longer endure it when a priest even takes the word "truth" into his mouth. Even with the most modest pretensions to uprightness, it *must* be known at present that a theologian, a priest, a pope, not only errs, but *lies,* with every sentence he speaks,—that he is no longer at liberty to lie out of "innocence," out of "ignorance." Even the priest knows as well as anyone knows that there is no longer any "God," any "sinner," any "Saviour;" that "free will" and a "moral order of the world" are *lies:*—seriousness, the profound self-surmounting of intellect, no longer allows anyone to be *ignorant* of these matters . . . *All* concepts of the Church have been recognised as what they are, as the wickedest of all forms of false coinage invented for the purpose of *depreciating* nature, natural values; the priest himself has been recognised as what he is, as the most dangerous species of parasite, as the actual poison-spider of life . . . We know, our *conscience* knows to-day—*what* those sinister inventions of the priests and of the Church are really worth, *what purpose was served* by those inventions by which that state of self-prostitution of mankind has been reached whose aspect can excite loathing—the concepts, "the other world," "last judgment," "immortality of soul," "soul" itself: they are torture instruments, they are systems of cruelty in virtue of which the priest became master, remained master . . . Everybody knows that; *and nevertheless everything remains in the old way*. What happened to the last sentiment of seemliness, of respect for ourselves, when our statesmen even, otherwise a very unbiassed species of men, and practical Anti-Christians through and through, call themselves Christians at the present day, and go to the communion? . . . A prince at the head of his regiments, splendid as the expression of the selfishness and elation of his nation,—but, *without* any shame, confessing himself a Christian! . . . *Whom* then does Christianity deny? *what* does it call the "world?" To be a soldier, a judge, a patriot; to defend one's self; to guard one's honour; to seek one's advantage; to be *proud* . . . All practice of every hour, all instincts, all valuations realising themselves in *deeds* are at present Anti-Christian: what a *monster of falsity* must modern man be that he nevertheless is *not ashamed* to be still called a Christian!——

39

I return, I repeat the genuine history of Christianity.—The very word "Christianity" is a misunderstanding;—in reality there has been only one Christian, and he died on the cross. The "Evangelium" *died* on the cross. What was called "Evangelium" from that hour onwards was already the antithesis of what *he* had lived: "*bad* tidings," a *Dysangelium*. It is false to the verge of absurdity, to see in a "belief" (perhaps in the belief of salvation through Christ) the distinguishing mark of the Christian: Christian *practice* alone (a life such as he who died on the cross *lived*) is Christian . . . At present *such* a life is still possible, for *certain* men it is even necessary: genuine, original Christianity will be possible at all times . . . *Not* a believing but a doing, a *not*-doing of many things, above all, a different existence . . . For states of consciousness, or any kind of believing, a taking-for-granted, for example,—as every psychologist knows,—are quite indifferent and of the fifth rank in comparison with the value of instincts: more strictly expressed: the whole concept of intellectual causality is false. To reduce the being a Christian, Christianness, to a taking-for-granted, to a mere phenomenality of consciousness, is to negative Christianness. *In fact there have never been Christians at all.* The "Christian," what for two millenniums has been called a Christian, is merely a psychological self-misunderstanding. Looked at more closely, it was *merely* the instincts which dominated in the Christian in spite of all his "belief"—and *what kind of instincts!*— "Belief" has been at all times (for example with Luther) only a cloak, a pretence, a *curtain* behind which the instincts played their game—a shrewd *blindness* with regard to the dominance of *certain* instincts . . . "Belief"—I already called it the peculiar Christian *shrewdness*,—

people always *spoke* about their "belief," but always *acted* merely from their instincts . . . In the world of concepts of the Christian nothing is contained which is in touch with actuality: on the other hand, we recognised in the instinctive hatred *of* all actuality, the motive element, the only motive element at the root of Christianity. What follows therefrom? That here, *in psychologicis* also, the error is radical, it is essence-determining, it is *substance*. A concept taken away here, a single reality put in its place—and the whole of Christianity tumbles into nothingness!—Looked at from an elevation, this strangest of all facts, a religion not only determined by errors, but inventive and even ingenious *only* in injurious, in life-poisoning and heart-poisoning errors, is a *spectacle for Gods*—for those Deities who are at the same time philosophers, and with whom I have met, for example, at those celebrated dialogues at Naxos. In the hour when the *loathing* leaves them (*and* us!), they become thankful for the spectacle of the Christian: the miserable, small star called earth deserves, perhaps, a divine glance, divine sympathy alone on account of *this* curious case . . . Do not let us undervalue the Christian: the Christian, false *even to innocence*, is far beyond the ape,—in respect to the Christian a well-known theory of descent becomes a mere compliment . . .

40

—The fate of the gospel was decided with the death,—it hung on the "cross" . . . It was only the death, the unexpected, disgraceful death, it was only the cross (which in general was reserved for the *canaille* alone), it was only this most awful paradox that brought the disciples face to face with the real enigma, "*Who was that? What was that?*"—The feeling staggered and profoundly insulted; the suspicion that such a death might be the *refutation* of their affair; the frightful question-mark: "Why just so?"—this condition is understood only too well. Here everything *had to* be necessary, everything *had to* have significance, reason, loftiest reason. The love of a disciple knows nothing of chance. It was now only that the chasm opened up: "Who killed him? Who was his natural enemy?"—this question came like a flash of lightning. Answer: *Domineering* Judaism, its upper class. From that moment they felt themselves in revolt *against* the established order, they afterwards understood Jesus as in *revolt against the established order*. Till then this combative characteristic, denying by word and deed, had been *absent* from his likeness; nay more, he had been the antithesis of it. Evidently the little community did *not* understand just the main thing, in what respect an example was set by dying in this manner, the freedom, the superiority *over* every feeling of *ressentiment*:—a sign how little they understood of him at all! In itself, Jesus could not wish aught by his death but to give publicly the strongest test, the *demonstration* of his doctrine . . . But his disciples were far from *forgiving* this death—which would have been evangelical in the highest sense,—and were equally far from *offering* themselves to a similar death in gentle and charming repose of heart . . . Just the most unevangelical of feelings, *revenge*, again came to the fore. It was deemed impossible that the affair could be at an end with this death: "recompense," "judgment" was needed (and yet, what can be more unevangelical than "recompense," "punishment," and "sitting in judgment?"). The popular expectation of a Messiah came once more into the foreground; an historical moment was seized by the eye: the "kingdom of God" comes for the judgment of his enemies . . . But everything is thereby misunderstood: the "kingdom of God" as a concluding act, as a promise! For the gospel had been precisely the existence, the fulfilment, the *actuality* of that kingdom. Such a death *was* just precisely that "kingdom of God" . . . It was now only that the whole of the contempt of, and bitterness against, the Pharisees and theologians was introduced into the type of the master,—he was thereby *made* a Pharisee and a theologian! On the other hand, the ensavaged reverence of these souls entirely disjointed did no longer endure the evangelical equal entitlement of everybody to be a child of God which Jesus had taught: their revenge was to *elevate* Jesus in an extravagant fashion, to sever him from themselves: quite in the same manner as the Jews had formerly separated their God from themselves and raised him aloft, for revenge on their enemies. The One God, and the One Son of God: both products of *ressentiment* . . .

41

—And from that time an absurd problem came to the surface: "How *could* God permit that!" With respect thereto the deranged reason of the little community found quite a frightfully absurd answer: God gave his Son for the forgiveness of sins, as a *sacrifice*. How it was all at once at an end with the gospel! The *sacrifice for guilt*, and just in its most repugnant and barbarous form, the sacrifice of the innocent for the sins of the guilty! What a horrifying heathenism!—For Jesus had done away with the concept of "guilt" itself—he denied that there was any gulf between man and God, he *lived* this unity of God and man as *his* "glad tidings" . . . And *not* as a privilege!—From that time onwards the type of the Saviour is entered progressively by the doctrine of judgment and of the second coming, by the doctrine of death as a sacrificial death, and by the doctrine of *resurrection*, with which the whole concept of blessedness, the entire and sole reality of the gospel, is filched away—

in favour of a state *after* death! . . . Paul, with the rabbinical impudence which distinguishes him in every respect, has brought reason into this concept, this *lewdness* of a concept, in the following way: "*If* Christ hath not been raised from the dead your faith is vain." — And all at once there arose out of the gospel the most contemptible of all unfulfillable promises, the *shameless* doctrine of personal immortality . . . Yet Paul himself taught it as a reward! . . .

<h2 style="text-align:center">42</h2>

One sees *what* came to an end with the death on the cross: a new, a thoroughly original commencement of a Buddhistic peace movement, of an actual and *not* merely promised *happiness on earth*. For this remains—I emphasised it before—the fundamental distinction between the two *décadence* religions: Buddhism gives no promise, but keeps every one; Christianity gives any promise, but *keeps none*.—The "glad tidings" were followed closely by the *worst of all*, those of Paul. In Paul, the antithetical type of the "bearer of glad tidings" is personified, the genius in hatred, in the vision of hatred, in the relentless logic of hatred. *What*, all has been sacrificed to hatred by this dysangelist! Above all the Saviour: Paul nailed the Saviour to *his own* cross. The life, the example, the teaching, the death, the significance, and the law of the entire gospel—nothing more was left when this false coiner by hatred conceived what he alone could use. *Not* reality, *not* historical truth! . . . And once more the priestly instinct of the Jew perpetrated the like great crime against history—it simply stroked out the yesterday, the day before yesterday of Christianity, it *invented for itself a history of first Christianity*. Yet more: it falsified the history of Israel over again in order to make it appear as a history preliminary to *its* achievement: all prophets are now supposed to have spoken of *its* "Saviour" . . . The Church later falsified even the history of mankind into a history preliminary to Christianity . . . The type of the Saviour, his teaching, his practice, his death, the significance of his death, even the sequel to his death—nothing remained untouched, nothing withal remained like the fact. Paul simply shifted the centre of gravity of that whole existence *behind* this existence,—into the *lie* of "risen" Jesus. In truth he could not use the life of the Saviour at all,—he needed the death on the cross, *and* something more besides . . . To take as honest a Paul (who had his home at the principal seat of Stoical enlightenment), when he derives from a hallucination the *proof* that the Saviour is yet living, or even to give credence to his account that he had had such a hallucination, would be a genuine *niaiserie* on the part of a psychologist: Paul willed the end, *consequently* he willed also the means . . . What he himself did not believe, was believed by the idiots among whom he cast *his* teaching.—*His* requirement was *power*; with Paul the priest strove once more for power,—he could only use concepts, doctrines, symbols, with which one tyrannises over masses and forms herds. What alone did Mohammed borrow later from Christianity? The invention of Paul, his expedient for priestly tyranny, for forming herds: the belief in immortality—*i.e. the doctrine of "judgment"* . . .

43

When the centre of gravity of life is placed, *not* in life, but in the "other world"—*in nothingness*—life has in reality been deprived of its centre of gravity. The great lie of personal immortality destroys all reason, all naturalness in instinct;—all that is beneficent, that is life-furthering, that pledges for the future in instincts, henceforth excites mistrust. So to live that it has no longer any *significance* to live, *that* now becomes the significance of life . . . For what purpose social sentiment, for what purpose to be still grateful for descent and for forefathers, for what purpose to co-operate, to trust, to further and have in view any general welfare? . . . Just so many temptations, just so many deviations from the "right path"—*"one thing* is needful" . . . That everyone, as an "immortal soul," has equal rank with everyone else, that in the universality of beings the salvation of *every* individual can lay claim to eternal importance, that little hypocrites and half-crazed people dare to imagine that on their account the laws of nature are constantly *broken*—such an enhancement of every kind of selfishness to infinity, to *impudence*, cannot be branded with sufficient contempt. And yet Christianity owes its *triumph* to this pitiable flattery of personal vanity,—it has thereby enticed over to its side all the ill-constituted, the seditiously disposed, the ill-fortuned, the whole scum and dross of humanity. "Salvation of the soul"—means, in plain words, "the world revolves around *me*" . . . The poison of the teaching of *"equal* rights for all"—has been spread abroad by Christianity more than by anything else, as a matter of principle; Christianity has, from the most secret recesses of bad instincts, waged a deadly war against every sentiment of reverence and distance between man and man, *i.e.* the *pre-requisite* to every elevation, to every growth of civilisation,—out of the *ressentiment* of the masses, it has forged for itself its *principal weapon* against *us*, against all that is noble, glad, and high-hearted on earth, against our happiness on earth . . . "Immortality" granted to every Peter and Paul, has hitherto been the worst, the most vicious outrage on *noble* humanity.—And let us not under-estimate the calamity which, proceeding from Christianity, has insinuated itself even into politics. At present nobody has any longer the courage for separate rights, for rights of domination, for a feeling of reverence for himself and his equals,—for *pathos of distance* . . . Our politics are *morbid* from this want of courage!—The aristocracy of character has been undermined most craftily by the lie of equality of souls; and if the belief in the "privilege of the many" makes revolutions and *will continue to make* them, it is Christianity, let us not doubt it, it is *Christian* valuations, which translate every revolution merely into blood and crime! Christianity is a revolt of all that creeps on the ground against what is *elevated*: the gospel of the lowly *makes* low . . .

44

—The Gospels are invaluable as evidence of the incessant corruption *within* the first congregation. What later was carried to an end by Paul with the logical cynicism of a rabbi, was, nevertheless, merely the process of decay which began with the death of the Saviour.—These Gospels cannot be read too guardedly: they have their difficulties behind every word. I confess—and I shall be pardoned for doing so—that to the psychologist they are just thereby a pleasure of the first rank, as the *antithesis* to all *naïve* depravity, as the refinement *par excellence*, as the artistic perfection in psychological depravity. The Gospels stand apart. The Bible in general does not admit of comparison: one is among Jews: the *chief* point of view, so as not to lose all consistency. The dissembling of one's self into "holiness," here becoming downright genius and never having been attained even approximately at any other time, either in books or among men, this false coinage in words and attitudes, as an *art*, is not the accident of any individual endowment, of any exceptional nature. *Race* is required for it. In Christianity, and its art of holy lying, Judaism entire, the most thoroughly earnest Jewish practice and technique of hundreds of years, attains its final masterliness. The Christian, this *ultima ratio* of the lie, is the Jew once more—even three times . . . The will to use, as a matter of principle, only concepts, symbols, and attitudes which are established by the praxis of the priest, the instinctive repudiation of every *other* praxis, of every *other* mode of perspective with regard to value and utility—that is not only tradition, it is *inheritance*: it is only as inheritance that it operates as nature. The whole human race, the best minds of the best ages even—one accepted, who is perhaps merely a monster—have been deceived. The Gospel has been read as the book of *innocence* . . . no small indication of the masterliness with which the game has been played here.—To be sure, if we should *see* them, only in passing, all these whimsical hypocrites and artificial saints, the end would have come,—and precisely because I never read a word with-

out perceiving attitudes. *I make an end of them* . . . I cannot endure a
certain way they have of opening their eyes.—Fortunately books are
for most people mere *literature*.—One must not be misled: "judge
not," they say, but they send everything to hell which stands in their
way. In making God judge, they themselves judge; in glorifying God,
they glorify themselves; in *demanding* those virtues of which they happen to be capable—yet more, which they need in order to get the better at all,—they assume the grand airs of a wrestling for virtue, of a
struggle for the triumph of virtue. "We live, we die, we sacrifice ourselves *for the good*" ("truth," "light," "the kingdom of God"): in fact,
they do what they cannot leave undone. In pressing themselves
through all kinds of holes, in sitting in the corner, in living like shadows in the shade, after the manner of sneaking creatures, they make a
duty out of it: their life in humility appears to be a duty; as humility, it
is an additional proof of their piety . . . Ah, this humble, chaste, char-
itable kind of falsehood! "For us virtue itself shall bear witness" . . . Let
the Gospels be read as books of seduction with morality: morality is ar-
rested by these wretched people,—they know of what consequence
morality is! Mankind is best *led by the nose* with morality!—The reality is that here the most conscious *self-conceit of the elect* plays the part
of discretion: they have placed *themselves*, the "congregation," the
"good and just," once for all on the one side, on the side of "truth,"—
and the others, "the world," on the other side . . . *That* has been the
most fatal species of ambitious monomania which has hitherto existed
on earth: wretched monsters of hypocrites and liars began to claim for
themselves the concepts "God," "truth," "light," "spirit," "love," "wisdom," "life," as if they were synonyms of them, in order to divide
themselves thus by a boundary-line from the "world,"—wretched su-
perlatives of Jews, ripe for every kind of mad-house, reversed the values altogether according to *their own nature*, as if only the Christian
was the significance, the salt, the standard, and even the *ultimate tribunal* for all the rest . . . The whole calamity became possible only by
a cognate, ethnologically cognate species of ambitious monomania,
Jewish monomania, being in the world: the gap between the Jews and
the Jewish Christians once opened up, no choice at all remained to
the latter except to apply the procedures for self-maintenance advised
by Jewish instinct, *against* the Jews themselves, while the Jews had
until then applied them only against all that was *not*-Jewish. The
Christian is but a Jew of "freer" confession.—

45

I give a few samples of what these wretched people have taken into their heads, what they *have put into the mouth* of their master: nothing but confessions of "beautiful souls."[1] —

"And whatsoever place shall not receive you, and they hear you not, as ye go forth thence, shake off the dust that is under your feet, for a testimony unto them. Verily, I say unto you, it shall be more tolerable for Sodom and Gomorrha in the day of judgment, than for that city." (Mark VI. 11.) — *How evangelical!* . . .

"And whosoever shall cause one of these little ones that believe on me to stumble, it were better for him if a great millstone were hanged about his neck, and he were cast into the sea." (Mark IX. 42.) — *How evangelical!* . . .

"And if thine eye cause thee to stumble, cast it out: it is good for thee to enter into the kingdom of God with one eye, rather than having two eyes to be cast into hell: where their worm dieth not, and the fire is not quenched." (Mark IX. 47.) — It is not quite the eye that is alluded to.

"Verily I say unto you, there be some here of them that stand by, which shall in no wise taste of death, till they see the kingdom of God come with power." (Mark IX. 1.) — Well *lied*, lion . . .

"If any man would come after me, let him deny himself, and take up his cross and follow me. *For*" . . . (*Remark of a Psychologist.* Christian morality is refuted by its *fors:* its reasons refute, — thus it is Christian.) Mark VIII. 34. —

"Judge not, *that* ye be not judged . . . with what measure ye mete, it shall be measured unto you." (Matthew VII. 1.) What a conception of justice, of a "just" judge! . . .

"For if ye love them that love you, *what reward have ye?* do not even the publicans the same? And if ye salute your brethren only, *what do ye more than others?* do not even the Gentiles the same?" (Matthew V. 46.) — Principle of Christian love: it wants to be well *paid* in the end . . .

"But if ye forgive not men their trespasses, neither will your Father forgive your trespasses." (Matthew VI. 15.) — Very compromising for the "Father" referred to . . .

"But seek ye first the kingdom of God and his righteousness, and all other things shall be added unto you." (Matthew VI. 33.) — All other things: namely, food, clothing, the whole necessaries of life. An *error*, modestly expressed . . . A little before, God appears as a tailor, at least in certain cases . . .

"Rejoice in that day and leap for joy: *for* behold, your reward is great in heaven: for in the same manner did their fathers unto the prophets." (Luke VI. 23.) — *Impudent* rabble! they already compare themselves to the prophets . . .

[1]An allusion to Goethe's "Bekenntnisse einer schönen Seele" in "Wilhelm Meister."

"Know ye not that ye are a temple of God, and that the Spirit of God dwelleth in you? If any man destroyeth the temple of God, *him shall God destroy*; for the temple of God is holy, *which temple ye are*." (Paul: I. Corinthians III. 16.)—Such utterances cannot be sufficiently despised . . .

"Or know ye not that the saints shall judge the world? and if the world is judged by *you*, are ye unworthy to judge the smallest matters?" (Paul: I. Corinthians VI. 2.)—Alas, not merely the talk of a bedlam . . . This *frightful deceiver* continues as follows: "Know ye not that *we* shall judge angels? how much more, things that pertain to this life?" . . .

"Hath not God made foolish the wisdom of the world? For seeing that in the wisdom of God, the world through its wisdom knew not God, it was God's good pleasure through the foolishness of the preaching to save them that believe . . . not many wise after the flesh, not many mighty, not many noble are called: but *God chose* the foolish things of the world, that he might put to shame them that are wise; and God chose the weak things of the world, that he might put to shame the things that are strong; and the base things of the world, and the things that are despised did God choose, yea, and the things that are not, that he might bring to naught the things that are: that no flesh should glory before God" (Paul: I. Corinthians I. 20 ff.)—For the purpose of *understanding* this passage, a document of the very first rank for the psychology of all Chandala morality,—the first essay of my *Genealogy of Morals* should be read: there for the first time the antithesis between a *noble* morality and a Chandala morality born out of *ressentiment* and impotent revenge, was brought forward. Paul was the greatest of all apostles of revenge . . .

46

—*What follows therefrom?* That one does well to put on gloves when reading the New Testament. The proximity of so much uncleanliness almost compels one to do so. We should as little choose "first Christians" for companionship as Polish Jews: not that even an objection was required against them . . . Neither of them have a good smell.—I have searched in vain in the New Testament for even a single sympathetic trait. There is nothing in it free, gracious, open-hearted, upright. Humanity has not yet made its beginning here,—the instincts of *cleanliness* are lacking . . . There are only bad instincts in the New Testament, there is no courage even for these bad instincts. All in it is cowardice, all is shutting of the eyes, and self-deception. Every book becomes cleanly, when one has just read the New Testament. To give an example, immediately after Paul, I read with delight Petronius, that most charming and wanton scoffer, of whom might be said what Domenico Boccaccio wrote to the Duke of Parma concerning Cesare Borgia: "*è tutto festo*"—immortally healthy, immortally cheerful and well-constituted . . . For these wretched hypocrites miscalculate in the main thing. They attack, but everything that is attacked by them is thereby *distinguished*. He who is attacked by a "first Christian" is *not* soiled . . . Reversely: it is an honour to have "first Christians" for enemies. The New Testament is not read without a predilection for that which is abused in it,—not to speak of the "wisdom of this world" which an impudent boaster in vain sought to put to shame by a "foolish sermon" . . . But even the Pharisees and scribes have an advantage from such antagonism: they must surely have been worth something to be hated in such an indecent manner. Hypocrisy—that is a reproach "first Christians" are allowed to make!—In the end the Pharisees and scribes were the *privileged:* that suffices, the Chandala hatred needs no further reasons. The "first Christian"—I fear also the last Christian, *whom I shall perhaps yet live to see*—is, by fundamental instinct, a rebel against everything privileged—he lives for, he struggles always for "equal rights!" . . . Examined more exactly, he has no choice. If one wants personally to be one of the "chosen of God" or a "temple of God," or a "judge of angels"—every *other* principle of selection, for example according to uprightness, according to intellect, according to manliness and pride, according to beauty and freedom of heart, is simply "world,"—*the evil in itself* . . . Moral: every expression in the mouth of a "first Christian" is a lie, every action he does is an instinctive falsehood—all his values, all his aims are injurious, but *he whom* he hates, *that* which he hates, *has value* . . . The Christian, the priestly Christian especially, is a *criterion of values.*——Have I yet to say that in the whole New Testament, only a *single* figure appears which one is obliged to honour?—Pilate, the Roman governor. To take a Jewish affair *seriously*—he will not be persuaded to do so. A Jew more or less—what does that matter? . . . The noble scorn of a Roman before whom a shameless misuse of the word "truth" was carried on has enriched the New Testament with the sole expression *which has value*,—which is itself its criticism, its *annihilation:* "What is truth!" . . .

47

—What separates *us* is not that we do not rediscover any God, either in history or in nature, or behind nature,—but that we recognise what was worshipped as God not as "divine," but as pitiable, as absurd, as injurious—not only as an error but as a *crime against life* . . . We deny God as God . . . If this God of the Christians were proved to us, we should still less know how to believe in him. — In a formula: *Deus qualem Paulus creavit, Dei negatio.* — A religion like Christianity, which is not in touch with actuality on any point, which immediately falls down as soon as actuality gets its right even in a single point, must, of course, be mortally hostile to the "wisdom of the world," *i.e.* to *science*, — it will approve of all expedients by which discipline of intellect, integrity and strictness in conscience-affairs of intellect, the noble coolness and freedom of intellect, can be poisoned, calumniated, and *defamed.* "Belief," as an imperative, is the *veto* against science, — *in praxi*, the lie at any price . . . Paul *understood* that the lie, the "belief," was needed; later the Church again understood Paul. — The God whom Paul devised, a God who "puts to shame the wisdom of the world" (in the narrower signification, the two great opponents of all superstition: philology and medicine), is in fact only the resolute *determination* of Paul himself to do so: to call "God" one's own will, *thora*, is truly Jewish. Paul *wants* to put to shame "the wisdom of the world;" his enemies are the *good* philologists and physicians of Alexandrian education, — it is against them that he wages war. In fact, nobody can be a philologist and physician without at the same time being an *Antichrist.* For a philologist looks *behind* the "holy books," a physician *behind* the physiological depravity of the typical Christian. The physician says, "incurable," the philologist says, "fraud" . . .

48

Has the celebrated story been really understood which stands at the commencement of the Bible, — the story of God's mortal terror of *science?* It has not been understood. This priest-book *par excellence* begins appropriately with the great inner difficulty of the priest: he has only one great danger, consequently "God" has only one great danger. —

The old God, entire "spirit," entire high priest, entire perfection, promenades in his garden: he only wants pastime. Against tedium even Gods struggle in vain.[1] What does he do? He contrives man, — man is entertaining . . . But behold, man also wants pastime. The pity of God for the only distress which belongs to all paradises has no bounds: he forthwith created other animals besides. The *first* mistake of God: man did not find the animals entertaining, — he ruled over them, but did not even want to be an "animal" — God consequently created woman. And, in fact, there was now an end of tedium, — but of other things also! Woman was the *second* mistake of God. — "Woman is in her essence a serpent, Hera" — every priest knows that: "from woman comes *all* the

---

[1] An allusion to Schiller's saying in the "Maid of Orléans": "Mit der Dummheit kämpfen Götter selbst vergebens."

mischief in the world"—every priest knows that likewise. *Consequently, science* also comes from her . . . Only through woman did man learn to taste of the tree of knowledge.—What had happened? The old God was seized by a mortal terror. Man himself had become his *greatest* mistake, he had created a rival, science makes *godlike;* it is at an end with priests and Gods, if man becomes scientific!—*Moral:* science is the thing forbidden in itself,—it alone is forbidden. Science is the *first* sin, the germ of all sin, *original* sin. *This alone is morality.*—"Thou shalt *not* know:"—the rest follows therefrom.—By his mortal terror God was not prevented from being shrewd. How does one *defend* one's self against science? That was for a long time his main problem. Answer: away with man, out of paradise! Happiness and leisure lead to thoughts,—all thoughts are bad thoughts . . . Man *shall* not think—and the "priest in himself" contrives distress, death, the danger of life in pregnancy, every kind of misery, old age, weariness, and above all *sickness,*—nothing but expedients in the struggle against science! Distress does not *permit* man to think . . . And nevertheless! frightful! the edifice of knowledge towers aloft, heaven-storming, dawning on the Gods,—what to do!—The old God contrives *war,* he separates the peoples, he brings it about that men mutually annihilate one another (the priests have always had need of war . . .). War, among other things, a great disturber of science!—Incredible! Knowledge, the *emancipation from the priest,* augments even in spite of wars.—And a final resolution is arrived at by the old God: "man has become scientific,—*there is no help for it, he must be drowned!*" . . .

49

—I have been understood. The beginning of the Bible contains the *entire* psychology of the priest.—The priest knows only one great danger: that is science,—the sound concept of cause and effect. But science flourishes on the whole only under favourable circumstances,—one must have *superfluous* time, one must have *superfluous* intellect in order to "perceive" . . . *Consequently* man must be made unfortunate,—this has at all times been the logic of the priest.—One makes out *what* has only thereby come into the world in accordance with this logic:—"sin" . . . The concepts of guilt and punishment, the whole "moral order of the world," have been devised *in opposition* to science,—*in opposition* to a severance of man from the priest . . . Man is *not* to look outwards, he is to look inwards into himself, he is *not* to look prudently and cautiously into things like a learner, he is not to look at all, he is to *suffer* . . . And he is so to suffer as to need the priest always.—Away with physicians! A *Saviour is needed.*—The concepts of guilt and punishment, inclusive of the doctrines of "grace," of "salvation," and of "forgiveness"—*lies* through and through, and without any psychological reality—have been contrived to destroy the *causal sense* in man, they are an attack on the concepts of cause and effect!—And *not* an attack with the fists, with the knife, with honesty in hate and love! But springing from the most cowardly, most deceitful, and most ignoble instincts! A *priest's* attack! A *parasite's* attack! A vampirism of pale, subterranean blood-suckers! When the natural consequences of a deed are no longer "natural," but are supposed to be brought about by the conceptual spectres of superstition, by "God," by "spirits," by "souls," as mere "moral" consequences, as reward, punishment, suggestion, or means of education, the pre-requisite of perception has been destroyed—*the greatest crime against mankind has been committed.* Sin, repeated once more, this form of human self-violation *par excellence*, has been invented for the purpose of making impossible science, culture, every kind of elevation and nobility of man; the priest *rules* by the invention of sin.—

50

—I do not, in this place, excuse myself from giving a psychology of "belief," of "believers," for the use—as is appropriate—of "believers." If to-day persons are still to be found who do not know in how far it is *indecent* to be a "believer"—or in how far it is a symbol of *décadence*, of a broken will to life,—they will know it by to-morrow. My voice reaches even those who are hard of hearing.—It appears, unless I have heard wrongly, that there is among Christians a kind of criterion of truth which is called "the proof by power." "Belief makes blessed, therefore it is true."—One might here object in the first place that the beautifying has not been proved, only *promised*: blessedness has been united with the condition of "believing,"—one *is to* become blessed—because one believes . . . But how could *that* be proved that what the priest promises to the believer for the "other world" inaccessible to all control, will actually happen?—The alleged "proof by power" is thus again, after all, only a belief that the effect, which is supposed to follow from belief, will not fail to take place. In a formula: "I believe that belief makes blessed;—*consequently*, it is true."—But here we are already at an end. The "consequently" would be the *absurdum* itself as a criterion of truth.—Granted however, with some obsequiousness, that the beautifying by belief be proved (*not* wished only, *not* promised only by the somewhat suspicious tongue of a priest), would blessedness—more technically expressed, *delight*—ever be a proof of truth? So little indeed that it almost furnishes the counter-proof; in any case the strongest suspicion against "truth" when feelings of delight have a voice in the question, "What is true?" The proof by "delight" is a proof for "delight,"—that is all. How is it established for all the world that *true* judgments give more enjoyment than false ones, and have, necessarily, according to a pre-established harmony, pleasant feelings in their train?—The experience of all stern, profoundly constituted intellects teaches *the reverse*. Every step towards truth has had to be fought for and there has had to be abandoned for it almost whatever otherwise human hearts, human love, human confidence in life, are attached to. Therefore greatness of soul is required: the service of truth is the hardest service.—What does it mean, then, to be *upright* in intellectual matters? To be stern with regard to one's heart, to despise "fine feelings," to make one's self a conscience out of every yea and nay!——Belief makes blessed: *consequently* it lies . . .

51

That belief under certain circumstances makes blessed, that bliss does not make a fixed idea *true*, that belief removes no mountains but *places* mountains where there are none: a hasty walk through a *madhouse* enlightens sufficiently on these matters. *Not* a priest to be sure: for he denies by instinct that sickness is sickness and a madhouse a madhouse. Christianity *needs* sickness, almost as Hellenism needs a surplus of healthfulness,—*making* sick is the true final purpose of the entire system of salvation-procedures of the Church. And the Church itself—is it not the Catholic madhouse as the ultimate ideal?—Earth as nothing but a madhouse?—Religious man, as the Church *wills* him to be, is a typical *décadent;* the period when a religious crisis becomes master of a people is always distinguished by nervous epidemics; the "inner world" of religious man is too similar to the "inner world" of the overexcited and exhausted for any distinction between the two; the "highest" states which Christianity has hung up over mankind as values of all values, are epileptoid manifestations.—*In majorem dei honorem* the Church has canonised nobody but crazed people *or* great deceivers . . . I once allowed myself to designate the whole Christian penitence-and-salvation-training (which can be studied best in England at present) as a *folie circulaire* methodically produced, of course upon a soil already prepared for it, *i.e.* a thoroughly morbid soil. Nobody is free to become a Christian: one is not "converted" to Christianity,—one must be morbid enough for it . . . We others, who have the *courage* for healthfulness *and* also for contempt, how *we* are permitted to despise a religion that teaches to misunderstand the body! that does not want to get rid of the superstition of the soul! that makes a "merit" of insufficient nourishment! that combats in healthfulness a sort of enemy, devil, or temptation! that persuaded itself, that a "perfect soul" could be carried about in a corpse of a body, and for that purpose needed to formulate a new concept of "perfection," a pale, sickly, idiotic-visionary essence, so-called "holiness,"—holiness, itself merely a series of symptoms of a body impoverished, enervated, and incurably ruined! . . . The Christian movement as a European movement, from the beginning, is a collective movement of all kinds of outcast and refuse elements (in Christianity that movement strives for power). It does *not* express the decay of a race, it is an aggregate formation of forms of *décadence* from everywhere which crowd together and seek one another. It was *not*, as is usually believed, the corruption of antiquity itself, of *noble* antiquity, that made Christianity possible: learned idiocy which even at present maintains such a belief cannot be contradicted with sufficient severity. At the time when the morbid, ruined Chandala classes of the whole *imperium* were christianised, the *countertype*, nobility, in precisely its finest and most mature form. The great number became master; the democratism of Christian instinct *conquered* . . . Christianity was not "national," it was not racially conditioned,—it appealed to every kind of persons disinherited of life, it had its allies everywhere. Christianity has at its basis the *rancune* of the sick, the instinct *opposed to* the healthy, *opposed to* healthfulness. Everything well-constituted, proud, high-spirited, and, above all, beauty, pains it in ear and eye. Once more I remind the reader of the invaluable expression of Paul: "the *weak* things of the world, the *foolish* things of the world, the *base* things of the world, and the things that are *despised*, did God choose:" that was the formula, *décadence* conquered *in hoc signo*.—*God on the cross*—is the frightful concept behind this symbol not as yet understood? All that suffers, all that hangs on the cross is divine . . . We all hang on the cross, consequently *we* are divine . . . We alone are divine . . . Christianity was a victory, a *nobler* type of character was destroyed by it,—Christianity has been the greatest misfortune hitherto of mankind.—

52

Christianity also stands in antithesis to all intellectual well-constitutedness, it can only use morbid reason as Christian reason, it takes the part of all the idiotic, it pronounces a curse against "intellect," against the *superbia* of sound intellect. Because sickness belongs to the essence of Christianity, the typical Christian state, "belief," *must* also be a form of sickness; all straight, upright, scientific paths to perception *must* be repudiated by the Church as forbidden paths. Doubt is already sin . . . The complete want of psychological cleanliness in the priest—betraying itself in his look—is a phenomenon *resulting from décadence,*—hysterical women, and children with rickety constitutions, must be observed in respect to the frequency with which instinctive falsity, delight in lying for the sake of lying, incapacity for looking straight and walking straight, are expressions of *décadence.* "Belief" means not-wishing-to-know what is true. The pietist, the priest of both sexes, is false *because* he is sick; his instinct is *averse* to truth having its rights on any point. "What makes sickly is *good;* what comes from fulness, from abundance, from power, is *evil:*" it is thus that the believer feels. *Constraint to lying*—I thereby discover every predetermined theologian.—Another mark of the theologian is his *incapacity for philology.* Under philology is here meant to be understood the art of reading well in a very general sense,—to be able to read off facts *without* falsifying them by interpretation, *without* losing precaution, patience, and acuteness in the desire to understand. Philology as *ephexis* in interpretation: whether books, newspapers, reports, events, or facts about the weather, be the matter,—not to speak of "salvation of the soul" . . . The way in which a theologian—it is all the same whether at Berlin or at Rome— explains an "expression of Scripture" or an experience, a victory of his country's troops, for example, under the higher illumination of the Psalms of David, is always so *daring* that it makes the philologist run up any wall. And what in the world is he to do when pietists and other cows from Swabia with the "finger of God" transform into a miracle of "grace," of "providence," or of "experience of salvation," the wretched common-place and chamber-smoke of their lives! The most modest expenditure of intellect, not to say of *propriety,* should certainly suffice to bring these interpreters to the conviction of the absolute childishness and unworthiness of such a misuse of divine manipulation. With ever so small an amount of piety in ourselves, a God who cures us of catarrh at the right time, or who bids us get into the carriage at the exact moment when a great rain commences, ought to be such an absurd God to us, that he would have to be done away with, even if he existed. God as a domestic servant, as a postman, as an almanac-maker,—after all, a word for the stupidest kind of accidents . . . "Divine providence," as it is still believed in by almost every third man in "educated Germany" would be such an objection to God that a stronger could not be thought of. And in any case, God is an objection to Germans! . . .

53

—It is so little true that *martyrs* prove anything as to the truth of an affair, that I would fain deny that ever a martyr has had anything to do with truth. By the tone in which a martyr throws at people's heads what he takes to be true, such a low grade of intellectual uprightness, such an *obtuseness* for the question of "truth" is expressed that a martyr never needs to be refuted. Truth is no thing which one person might have and another might lack: thus, at the best, peasants, or peasant-apostles like Luther, can think concerning truth. One may be sure that proportionally to the grade of conscientiousness in intellectual matters, modesty, *resignation* on this point always becomes greater. To *know* concerning five matters, and with dainty hand to decline to know *anything else* . . . "Truth," as the word is understood by every prophet, every sectary, every freethinker, every socialist, every churchman, is a complete proof that as yet there has not even a beginning been made with the intellectual discipline and self-overcoming which are needed for the finding of any small, ever so small truth.—The martyr-deaths, to say a word in passing, have been a great misfortune in history: they have *seduced* . . . The inference of all idiots, women and mob included, to the effect that an affair for which anyone lays down his life (or which, like primitive Christianity, even produces death-seeking epidemics) is of importance,—this inference has become an unspeakable drag upon verification, upon the spirit of verification and precaution. The martyrs have *injured* truth . . . Even at present a crude form of persecution is all that is needed to create an *honourable* name for a sectarianism ever so indifferent in itself.—What! does it alter anything in the value of an affair that somebody lays down his life for it?—An error which becomes honourable is an error which possesses an additional seductive charm: do you think we would give you an opportunity, Messrs. the theologians, of being the martyrs for your lie? One refutes a thing by laying it respectfully on ice,—it is just so that one refutes theologians also . . . It was just the grand historical stupidity of all persecutors that they gave an honourable aspect to the cause of their opponents,—that they made a present to it of the fascination of martyrdom . . . Woman is still prostrate on her knees before an error, because she has been told that somebody has died for it on the cross. *Is the cross then an argument?*—— But with regard to all these matters one alone has said the word that has been needed for millenniums,—*Zarathushtra.*

Signs of blood have been written by them on the way they went, and it was taught by their folly that truth is proved by blood.

But blood is the worst of all witnesses for truth; blood poisoneth even the purest teaching and turneth it into delusion and hatred of hearts.

And when a man goeth through fire for his teaching—what is proved thereby? Verily, it is more when one's own teaching springeth from one's own burning.

54

Let nobody be led astray: great intellects are sceptical. Zarathushtra is a sceptic. Strength, *freedom* derived from the force and over-force of intellect is *proved* by scepticism. Men of conviction do not even count in determining what is fundamental in value and not-value. Convictions are prisons. Such men do not see far enough, they do not see *below* themselves: but to be permitted to have a voice concerning value and not-value, one must see five hundred convictions *below* one's self, — *behind* one's self . . . An intellect which wills what is great, which wills also the means to it, is necessarily sceptical. The freedom from every kind of conviction, the *ability* to look freely, *belong* to strength . . . Grand passion, the basis and power of a sceptic's existence, still more enlightened, still more despotic than himself, takes his entire intellect into service; it makes him unscrupulous, it gives him courage even for unholy means; under certain circumstances it does not grudge to him convictions. Conviction as a *means:* Many things are attained only by means of conviction. Grand passion uses, uses up convictions, it does not subject itself to them — it knows itself sovereign. — Reversely, the need of a belief, of something that is unconditioned by yea or nay, Carlylism, if I shall be pardoned the word, is a requirement of *weakness.* The man of belief, the "believer" of every kind, is necessarily a dependent man, — one who cannot posit *himself* as an end, who cannot out of himself posit ends at all. The "believer" does not belong to *himself,* he can only be a means, he must be *used up,* he needs somebody who will use him up. His instinct gives the highest honour to a morality of self-abnegation: everything persuades him to it, his shrewdness, his experience, his vanity. Every kind of belief is itself an expression of self-abnegation, of self-estrangement . . . If it be considered how necessary for most people is a regulative which binds them from the outside and makes them fast; as coercion, *slavery* in a higher sense, is the sole and ultimate condition under which the weak-willed human being, especially woman, flourishes, — conviction, "belief," are understood. The man of conviction has it for his backbone. *Not* to see many things, to be nowhere unbiassed, to be an interested party through and through, to have strict and necessary optics with regard to all values — these alone are the conditions for such a kind of man existing. But he is thereby the antithesis, the *antagonist* of the truthful, of truth . . . The believer is not at liberty to have at all a conscience for the questions of "true" and "untrue;" to be upright *here* would be his immediate ruin. Pathological conditionedness of his optics makes a fanatic out of a convinced person — Savonarola, Luther, Rousseau, Robespierre, Saint-Simon, — the type antithetical to the strong, *emancipated* intellect. But the strong attitude of these *morbid* intellects, these conceptual epileptics, operates on the great mass—the fanatics are picturesque, mankind prefers seeing postures to hearing *reasons* . . .

55

A step further in the psychology of conviction, of "belief." It is now a long time since the question was submitted by me for consideration, whether convictions are not more dangerous enemies of truth than falsehoods (Human, All-too-Human, I. Aph. 483). This time I should like to ask the decisive question: does there exist at all an antithesis between falsehood and conviction?—All the world believes it; but what is not believed by all the world?—Every conviction has its history, its previous forms, its tentatives and mistakes; its *becomes* conviction after for a long time *not* having been so, after for a yet longer time having *hardly* been so. What? could not falsehood also be among these embryonic forms of conviction?—It sometimes needs merely a change of persons: that in the son becomes conviction which in the father was still falsehood.—*Not* wishing to see something which one sees, not wishing *so* to see something as one sees it: that is what I call falsehood: it does not matter whether or not the falsehood takes place in presence of witnesses. The commonest falsehood is that by which one deceives one's self; the deception of others is a relatively exceptional case.—Now this *not*-wishing-to-see what one sees, this not-wishing-*so*-to-see as one sees, is almost the first condition for all who are *party* in any sense whatsoever; the party-man becomes a liar by necessity. German historiography, for example, is convinced that Rome was despotism, that the Germanics brought the spirit of freedom into the world: what is the difference between this conviction and a falsehood? Need one yet wonder if, by instinct, all parties (inclusive of German historians) have the sublime words of morality in their mouths,—that morality almost *continues to exist* owing to party-men of all kinds having need of it every hour?— "This is *our* conviction: we confess it before all the world, we live and die for it.—Respect all that have convictions!"—I have heard the like even out of the mouths of Anti-Semites. On the contrary, gentlemen! An Anti-Semite does by no means become more decent because he lies on principle . . . The priests, who in such matters are more refined and understand very well the objection which lies in the concept of a conviction (*i.e.* a mendacity that is axiomatic, *because* it serves the purpose), have obtained from the Jews the policy of inserting in this place the concepts "God," "will of God," "revelation of God." Kant also, with his categorical imperative, was on the same road: his reason became *practical* in this matter.—There are questions in which the decision concerning truth or untruth does *not* appertain to man; all highest questions, all highest problems of value are beyond human reason . . . To understand the limits of reason, — *that* only is genuine philosophy . . . For what end did God give man revelation? Would God have done anything superfluous? Man *cannot* know of himself what is good and evil; on that account God taught him his will . . . Moral: the priest does *not* lie, — the question of "true" or "untrue," in such matters as priests speak about, does not even permit of lying. For in order to be able to lie one would require to be able to determine *what* is true here. But that is just what man *cannot* do; the priest is thereby only the mouth-piece of God. — Such a priestly syllogism is by no means exclusively Jewish or Christian; the right of lying and the *policy* of "revelation" belong to the type of the priest, to the priests of *décadence* as well as of heathendom (heathens are all who say yea to life, to whom "God" is the word for the great yea to everything). — "Law," "will of God," the "holy book," "inspiration," — all only words for the conditions *under* which the priest attains to power, *by* which he maintains his power; — these concepts are found at the basis of every organisation of priests, of every hierarchic or philosopho-hierarchic structure. "Holy falsehood" — common to Confucius, to the Law-book of Manu, to Mohammed, to the Christian Church, — it is not absent in Plato. "Truth is here:" that means wherever it becomes audible, *the priest lies* . . .

56

— Finally it is of moment, for what *end* there is lying. That in Christianity "holy" ends are lacking is *my* objection to its means. Only *bad* ends, poisoning, calumniating, and denying of life, despising of body, abasement and self-violation of man through the concept of sin — *consequently* its means also are bad. — With an entirely different feeling, I read the Law-book of Manu, an incomparably intellectual and superior work, which it would be a sin against the *spirit* even to *name* in the same breath with the Bible. It appears at once: it has an actual philosophy behind it, in it, not a mere bad-smelling Jewish acid of rabbinism and superstition, — it gives even to the most dainty psychologist something to bite at. Not to forget the main thing, the fundamental difference from every kind of Bible: the *noble* classes, the philosophers, and the warriors by means of it stretch out their hands over the multitude; noble values everywhere, a feeling of perfection, an affirmation of life, a triumphing agreeable sensation in one's self and in life, — *sunshine* spreads over the entire book. — All the things which Christianity takes for objects of its unfathomable vulgarity, for example procreation, woman, marriage, are here treated seriously, with reverence, love, and confidence. How can one really put a book into the hands of children and women which contains those vile words: "Because of fornications let each man have his own wife, and let each woman have her own husband . . . for it is better to marry than to burn?" And is it *allowable* to be a Christian as long as the origin of man is christianised, *i.e. befouled* with the concept of *immaculata conceptio?* . . . I know of no book in which so many delicate and kind things are said of woman as in the Law-book of Manu; those old grey beards and saints have a mode of being gracious towards women, which perhaps has not been surpassed. "The mouth of a woman," the book says once,—"the bosom of a maiden, the prayer of a child, the smoke of sacrifice, are ever pure." Another passage: "There is nothing purer than the light of the sun, the shadow of a cow, air, water, fire, and the breath of a maiden." A last passage—perhaps also a holy lie: "All openings of the body above the navel are pure, all under it are impure. In a maiden only the whole body is pure."

57

The *unholiness* of Christian means is surprised *in flagrante*, when for once the *Christian end* is measured by the end of the Law-book of Manu,—when this greatest antithesis of ends is put under a strong light. The critic of Christianity cannot help making Christianity *contemptible.*—Such a law-book as that of Manu originates like every good law-book: it sums up the experience, the policy and the experimental morality of long centuries; it finishes, it no longer creates. The pre-requisite for a codification of that kind is the insight that the means for creating authority for a *truth* slowly and expensively acquired, are fundamentally different from those with which one would prove it. A law-book never recounts the advantage, the reasons, the casuistry in the previous history of a law: it would just thereby lose its imperative tone, the "thou shalt," the pre-requisite for its being obeyed. The problem lies exactly in this.—At a certain point in the development of a nation, its most circumspect class (*i.e.* the most retrospective and prospective) declares the experience to be closed according to which people are to live—*i.e.* according to which they *can* live.—Its aim is to bring home from the times of experiment and *unfortunate* experience the richest and completest harvest possible. Consequently, what is above all to be avoided, is the continuation of experimenting, the continuation of the fluid condition of values, testing, choosing, and criticising of values *in infinitum.* A double wall is established in opposition to this: on the one hand *revelation, i.e.* the assertion that the reason of those laws is *not* of human origin, *not* wearisomely sought out and found after many mis-

takes, but of divine origin, entire, perfect, without a history,—a be-
stowal, a miracle, a mere communication . . . On the other hand *tradition, i.e.* the assertion that the law has already existed since primitive
times, that it is impious, that it is a crime against the ancestors, to call
it in question. The authority of the law is established by the theses: God
gave it, the ancestors *lived* under it.—The higher reason of such pro-
cedure consists in the design to thrust back the consciousness step by
step from the mode of life recognised as correct (*i.e. proved* by an experience immense and sharply sifted), so that a perfect automatism of
instinct is attained,—the pre-requisite for every kind of masterliness, for
every kind of perfection in the art of life. To draw up a law-book like
that of Manu means the concession to a people to become in future
masterly, perfect,—to exercise ambition for the highest art of life. *For
that end it must be made unconscious:* that is the object of all holy falsehood.—The order of castes, the highest, the dominating law, is only the
sanction of an *order of nature,* natural lawfulness of the first rank, over
which no arbitrariness, no "modern idea," has power. In every healthy
society, three types, mutually conditioning and differently gravitating,
physiologically separate themselves, each of which has its own hygiene,
its own domain of labour, its own special sentiment of perfection, its
own special mastership. Nature, *not* Manu, separates from one another
the mainly intellectual individuals, the individuals mainly excelling in
muscular strength and temperament, and the third class neither distinguished in the one nor in the other, the mediocre individuals,—the
latter as the great number, the former as the select individuals. The
highest caste—I call them the *fewest*—has, as the perfect caste, the
privileges of the fewest: it belongs thereto to represent happiness,
beauty, goodness on earth. Only the most intellectual men have the
permission to beauty, *to* the beautiful; it is only with them that goodness is not weakness. *Pulchrum est paucorum hominum:* the good is a
privilege. On the other hand, nothing can be less permissible to them
than unpleasant manners or a pessimistic look, an eye that *makes deformed,*—or even indignation with regard to the entire aspect of things.
Indignation is the privilege of the Chandala; and pessimism similarly.
"The world is perfect"—thus speaks the instinct of the most intellectual
men, affirmative instinct; "imperfection, every kind of *inferiority* to us,
distance, pathos of distance, even the Chandala belong to this perfection." The most intellectual men, as the *strongest,* find their happiness
in that in which others would find their ruin: in the labyrinth, in severity towards themselves and others, in effort; their delight is self-
overcoming: with them asceticism becomes naturalness, requirement,
instinct. A difficult task is regarded by them as a privilege, to play with
burdens which crush others to death, as a *recreation* . . . Knowledge, a

form of asceticism.—They are the most venerable kind of man. That does not exclude their being the most cheerful, the most amiable. They rule, not because they will, but because they *are*; they are not at liberty to be the second in rank.—The *second* in rank are: the guardians of right, the keepers of order and security, the noble warriors, the *king*, above all, as the highest formula of warrior, judge, and keeper of the law. The second in rank are the executive of the most intellectual, the most closely associated with them, relieving them of all that is *coarse* in the work of ruling, their retinue, their right hand, their best disciples.— In all that, to repeat it once more, there is nothing arbitrary, nothing "artificial;" what is *otherwise* is artificial,—by what is otherwise, nature is put to shame . . . By the order of castes, the *order of rank*, the supreme law of life itself is formulated only; the separation of the three types is necessary for the maintenance of society, for the making possible of higher and highest types,—the *inequality* of rights is the very condition of there being rights at all.—A right is a privilege. In his mode of exis- tence everyone has his privilege. Let us not undervalue the privileges of the *mediocre*. Life always becomes harder towards the *summit*,—the cold increases, responsibility increases. A high civilisation is a pyramid: it can only stand upon a broad basis, it has for a first pre-requisite a strongly and soundly consolidated mediocrity. Handicraft, trade, agri- culture, *science*, the greater part of art, in a word, the whole compass of business activity, is exclusively compatible with an average amount of ability and pretension; the like pursuits would be displaced among the exceptions, the instinct appropriate thereto would contradict aristo- cratism as well as anarchism. There is a determination of nature that a person should be a public utility, a wheel, a function: *not* society, the kind of *happiness* of which alone the larger number are capable, makes intelligent machines out of them. For the mediocre, it is a happiness to be mediocre; for them the mastery in one thing, specialism, is a natural instinct. It would be altogether unworthy of a profounder intellect to see in mediocrity itself an objection. It is indeed the *first* necessity for the possibility of exceptions: a high civilisation is conditioned by it. If the exceptional man just treats the mediocre with a more delicate touch than himself and his equals, it is not mere courtesy of heart,—it is simply his *duty* . . . Whom do I hate most among the mob of the pres- ent day? The Socialist mob, the Chandala apostles, who undermine the working man's instinct, his pleasure, his feeling of contentedness with his petty existence,—who make him envious, who teach him re- venge . . . The wrong never lies in unequal rights, it lies in the preten- sion to "*equal*" rights . . . What is *bad*? But I said it already: all that springs from weakness, from envy, from *revenge*.—The anarchist and the Christian are of the same origin . . .

58

In fact it makes a difference for what object a person lies: whether he thereby preserves or *destroys*. One may institute a perfect equation between the *Christian* and the *anarchist*: their object, their instinct is towards destruction. The proof of this proposition can be read plainly from history,—it is contained in history with frightful distinctness. If we just became acquainted with a religious legislation whose object was to make eternal the highest condition for making life *flourish*, a great organisation of society,—Christianity, on the other hand, found its mission in putting an end to just such an organisation, *because life flourished in it.* There the proceeds of reason from long periods of experiment and uncertainty were intended to be invested for the most remote advantage, and the harvest was intended to be brought home as large, as rich, and as complete as possible: here, reversely, the harvest was *blighted* during the night . . . That which stood there *ære perennius*, the *imperium Romanum*, the grandest form of organisation under difficult conditions that has hitherto been realised, in comparison with which everything previous, everything subsequent, is patchwork, bungling, and dilettanteism,—those holy anarchists have made a "piety" out of destroying "the world," *i.e.* the *imperium Romanum*, until no stone remained upon another,—until even Germanics and other boors could become master over it . . . The Christian and the anarchist: both *décadents*, both incapable of operating otherwise than disintegrating, blighting, stunting, *blood-sucking*, both incarnating the instinct of *mortal hatred* of whatever stands, whatever is great, whatever has durability, whatever promises futurity to life. Christianity was the vampire of the *imperium Romanum*,—in the night it has undone the immense achievement of the Romans, of obtaining the site for a grand civilisation that would *require time.*—Is it not yet understood? The *imperium Romanum* which we know, which the history of the Roman province always teaches us to know better, that most admirable work of art of the grand style, was a commencement, its structure was calculated to *prove* itself by millenniums,—hitherto there has never been such building, no building in like magnitude *sub specie æterni* has even been dreamt of!—That organisation was steadfast enough to endure bad emperors: the accident of persons must have nothing to do in such matters,—*first* principle of all great architecture. But it was not steadfast enough against the *corruptest* kind of corruption, against the *Christian* . . . These stealthy vermin which, in darkness, obscurity, and duplicity, approached every individual, sucking out of him the seriousness for *true* things, the entire instinct for *realities*; that cowardly, feminine, and honeyed crew have gradually estranged the "souls" from that immense edifice,—those valuable, those manly, noble natures, who felt the affair of Rome to be their own affair, their own seriousness, their own *pride*. Hypocrite-sneaking, conventicle-stealthiness, gloomy concepts such as hell, sacrifice of the innocent, *unio mystica* in blood-drinking, above all the slowly stirred up fire of revenge, of Chandala revenge—*that* became master over Rome, the same kind of religion against the pre-existent form of which Epicurus had waged war. Let a person read Lucretius to understand *what* Epicurus combated, *not* heathenism, but "Christianity," *i.e.* the depravity of souls by the concepts of guilt, punishment, and immortality.—He combated the *subterranean* cults, the whole latent Christianity;—to deny immortality was then an actual *salvation*.—And Epicurus would have conquered; every respectable intellect in the Roman Empire was Epicurean: *then Paul appeared* . . . Paul, the incarnated, genius-inspired Chandala hatred against Rome, against the world,—the Jew, the eternal Jew *par excellence* . . . What he found out was how to light a "universal conflagration" by the aid of the small sectarian Christian movement apart from Judaism, how to sum up to a prodigious power by the symbol of "God on the cross" all the inferior, all the secretly seditious, the whole heirship of the anarchist intrigues in the Empire. "Salvation is of the Jews."—Christianity as a formula for outbidding—*and* summing up—all kinds of subterranean cults, like those of Osiris, of the Great Mother, of Mithra, for example: Paul's genius consists in discerning this. His instinct was so certain therein that, with regardless violence to truth, he put the ideas with which those Chandala religions fascinated into the mouth of the "Saviour" of his own invention, and not only into the mouth—that he *made* out of him something which a Mithra-priest also could understand. That was his moment of Damascus: he understood that he *needed* the belief in immortality in order to depreciate "the world," that the concept of "hell" becomes even master of Rome,—that *life* is killed by the "other world" . . . Nihilist and Christian: they rhyme in German, and do not rhyme only . . .

59

The whole labour of the ancient world *in vain*: I have no words to express my sentiments with regard to a thing so hideous.—And in consideration that its work was a preparation, that only the substructure was laid with granite self-consciousness for the work of millenniums, the entire *meaning* of the ancient world in vain! . . . For what end the Greeks? for what end the Romans?—All pre-requisites to a learned civilisation, all scientific *methods* were already there, the great, the incomparable art of reading well had already been established—that pre-requisite to the tradition of civilisation, to the unity of science; natural science in alliance with mathematics and mechanics were on the best of all paths,—the *sense for fact*, the last and most valuable of all senses, had its schools and its tradition already centuries old! Is that understood? Everything *essential* had been discovered to enable people to go to work: the methods, it must be repeated ten times, *are* the essential thing, also the most difficult thing, and besides the things that have habit and indolence longest against them. What we have now won back for ourselves with unspeakable self-vanquishing (for we have still somehow all bad instincts, Christian instincts in our nature)—the open look in presence of reality, the cautious hand, patience and earnestness in details, all the *righteousness* in knowledge,—it was already there! already, more than two thousand years ago! *And* added thereto, the excellent, refined tact and taste! *Not* as brain drilling! *Not* as "German" culture with boorish manners! But as body, as bearing, as instinct,—in a word, as reality . . . *All in vain!* Ere the morrow, merely a memory!— The Greeks! The Romans! Nobility of instinct, taste, methodical investigation, genius for organisation and administration, belief in, *will* to the future of man, the great yea to all things visible as *imperium Romanum*, visible to all senses, the grand style, no longer merely art, but become reality, truth, *life* . . .—And choked in the night, not by any natural accident! Not trampled down by Germanics and other heavy-footed—creatures! But put to shame by crafty, secretive, invisible, anæmic vampires! Not conquered,—only sucked out! . . . Hidden vindictiveness, petty envy become *master!* Everything wretched, suffering from itself, visited by bad feelings, the entire *Ghetto world* of soul, *uppermost* all at once!——One has but to read any Christian agitator, Saint Augustine for instance, to be able to *smell* what dirty fellows have thereby got uppermost. One would be thoroughly deceived by presupposing any want of understanding in the leaders of the Christian movement:—oh, they are shrewd, shrewd even to holiness, Messrs. the Fathers of the Church! What they lack is something quite different. Nature neglected them,—it forgot to give them a modest dowry of respectable, decent, *cleanly* instincts . . . In confidence, they are not even men . . . If Islam despises Christianity it has a thousand times the right to do so: Islam has *men* for a pre-requisite . . .

60

Christianity has made us lose the harvest of ancient civilisation, it has again, later, made us lose the harvest of Islam civilisation. The wonderful world of Moorish civilisation of Spain, on the whole nearer akin to *us*, speaking more to sense and taste than Rome and Greece, was *trampled down* (I do not say by what sort of feet), why? because it owed its origin to noble, to manly instincts, because it said yea to life, even with the rare and refined jewels of Moorish life! . . . The crusaders, later, combated something before which it might have been more becoming for them to lie in the dust,—a civilisation in comparison with which even our nineteenth century might appear to itself very poor, very "late." To be sure, they wanted to gain booty: the Orient was rich . . . Let us not be biassed! Crusades—superior piracy, that is all. German nobility, a Viking nobility at bottom, was there in its element: the Church knew only too well by what German nobility is attracted . . . The German noble, always the "Swiss guard" of the Church, always in the service of all bad instincts of the Church, but *well paid* . . . That the Church, just with the aid of German swords, German blood and courage, has carried through its mortally hostile warfare against everything noble upon earth! There are at this place a great number of painful questions. German nobility is scarcely to be *met with* in the history of higher civilisation: the reason is obvious . . . Christianity, alcohol—the two *great* means of corruption . . . For in itself, there should be no choice in the face of Islam and Christianity, as little as in the face of an Arab and a Jew. The decision is given; nobody is still free to choose here. Either a person *is* a Chandala, or he is *not* . . . War to the knife with Rome! Peace, friendship with Islam: it was thus that the great free spirit, the genius among the German emperors, Frederick II felt, it was thus that he *did*. What? has a German to be first a genius, to be first a free spirit in order to feel *becomingly*? I do not understand how a German could ever feel *Christian* . . .

61

Here it is necessary to touch upon a reminiscence a hundred times more painful to Germans. The Germans have caused Europe the loss of the last great harvest of civilisation that was to be garnered for Europe—the *Renaissance*. Is it at last understood, is it *desired* to be understood *what* the Renaissance was? The *transvaluation of Christian values*, the attempt, undertaken with all means, with all instincts, with all genius, to bring about the triumph of the *opposite* values, the *noble* values . . . There has only been *this* great war hitherto, there has hitherto been no more decisive question than the Renaissance,—*my* question is *its* question: neither has there ever been a form of attack more fundamental, more direct, more strenuously delivered with a whole front upon the centre of the enemy! To attack at the most decisive place, at the seat of Christianity itself, to set in this respect upon the throne the noble values, *i.e.* to *introduce* them into the most radical requirements and longings of those sitting there . . . I see before me the *possibility* of a perfectly supernatural enchantment and colour charm: it seems to me to shine in all tremors of refined beauty, that there is an art at work in it, so divine, so devilishly divine, that one might for millenniums seek in vain for a second example of such a possibility; I see a spectacle so ingenious, so wonderfully paradoxical at the same time, that all Divinities of Olympus would have had an occasion for an immortal laughter—*Cesare Borgia as Pope* . . . Am I understood? Well, *that* would have been the triumph for which *I* alone am longing at present; Christianity would thereby have been *done away with!* What happened? A German monk, Luther, came to Rome. This monk, with all the vindictive instincts of an abortive priest in his nature, became furious *against* the Renaissance in Rome . . . Instead of, with the profoundest gratitude, understanding the prodigy that had taken place, the overcoming of Christianity at its *seat,*—his hatred only knew how to draw its nourishment from this spectacle. A religious person thinks only of himself.—Luther saw the *depravity* of Popery, while the very reverse was palpable: the old depravity, the *peccatum originale*, Christianity, no longer sat on the throne of the Pope! But life! The triumph of life! The great yea to all things high, beautiful, and daring! . . . And Luther *restored the Church once more:* he attacked it . . . The Renaissance—an event without meaning, a great *in-vain!*—Ah those Germans, what they have already cost us! In-vain—that has ever been the *work* of the Germans.—The Reformation; Leibniz; Kant and so-called German philosophy; the wars of "Liberation;" the Empire— every time an in-vain for something that had already existed, for something *irrecoverable* . . . They are *my* enemies, I confess it, these Germans. In despising them I despise every kind of uncleanliness in concepts and valuations, every kind of *cowardice* in presence of every straight-forward yea and nay. They have felted and confused, for a thousand years almost, whatever they laid their fingers on, they have on their conscience all the halfnesses—the three-eighthnesses!—from which Europe is sick,—they have also on their conscience the foulest kind of Christianity, the most incurable, the most irrefutable that exists, Protestantism . . . If we do not get done with Christianity, the *Germans* will be to blame for it . . .

62

—With this I am at the conclusion and pronounce my sentence. I condemn *Christianity*, I bring against the Christian Church the most terrible of all accusations that ever an accuser has taken into his mouth. It is to me the greatest of all imaginable corruptions, it has had the will to the ultimate corruption that is at all possible. The Christian Church has left nothing untouched with its depravity, it has made a worthlessness out of every value, a lie out of every truth, a baseness of soul out of every straight-forwardness. Let a person still dare to speak to me of its "humanitarian" blessings! To *do away with* any state of distress whatsoever was counter to its profoundest expediency, it lived by states of distress, it *created* states of distress in order to perpetuate *itself* eternally . . . The worm of sin for example; it is only the Church that has enriched mankind with this state of distress!—The "equality of souls before God," this falsehood, this *pretence* for the *rancunes* of all the base-minded, this explosive material of a concept which has finally become revolution, modern idea, and *décadence* principle of the whole order of society—is *Christian* dynamite . . . "Humanitarian" blessings of Christianity! To breed out of *humanitas* a self-contradiction, an art of self-violation, a will to the lie at any price, a repugnance, a contempt for all good and straight-forward instincts! Those are for me blessings of Christianity!—Parasitism as the *sole* praxis of the Church; drinking out all blood, all love, all hope for life, with its anæmic ideal of holiness; the other world as the will to the negation of every reality; the cross as the rallying sign for the most subterranean conspiracy that has ever existed,—against healthiness, beauty, well-constitutedness, courage, intellect, *benevolence* of soul, *against life itself* . . .

This eternal accusation of Christianity I shall write on all walls, wherever there are walls,—I have letters for making even the blind see . . . I call Christianity the one great curse, the one great intrinsic depravity, the one great instinct of revenge for which no expedient is sufficiently poisonous, secret, subterranean, *mean*,—I call it the one immortal blemish of mankind . . .